TREATMENT
EFFECTIVENESS
HANDBOOK

TREATMENT
EFFECTIVENESS
HANDBOOK

A reference guide to
the key research reviews
in mental health and
substance abuse

Howard B. Pikoff
State University of New York at Buffalo

DATA FOR DECISIONS
Buffalo   New York

Notice to Readers

Every effort has been made to accurately represent the findings, opinions and conclusions of the reviews and studies which are summarized in this book. However, since all such findings, opinions and conclusions are subject to differing interpretations, as well as to unintentional misrepresentation due to human or mechanical error, it is the responsibility of the reader to directly examine the reviews cited and the original studies to which they refer. Furthermore, since therapeutic standards may change as research and practice advance, and in response to the facts of a particular case, readers are advised to follow the treatment recommendations of the health care provider who is directly responsible for their care. Neither the publisher nor the author make any warranties concerning the information in this book or its subsequent use.

This book is printed on acid-free paper.

DATA FOR DECISIONS
50 Chatham Avenue Buffalo, New York 14216-3109

Library of Congress Catalog
Card Number 96-84425   ISBN 0-9640981-0-5

Many thanks to Linda Gould, Michele McCormick, & Craig Dickinson.

Printed in the United States of America

For Ann, Emily, and Rebecca

CONTENTS

OVERVIEW

SCOPE

This handbook contains summaries and analysis of 242 clinical research reviews published in the preeminent journals of mental health and substance abuse. Each review synthesizes the results of sometimes dozens, sometimes hundreds of individual clinical trials. Taken together, they provide a gateway to the findings of five decades of treatment effectiveness research.

More than 20 clinical procedures are represented, ranging from psychoanalysis and cognitive therapy to biofeedback and eye-movement desensitization. Selected pharmacotherapy reviews are also included which address the effectiveness of drug treatment relative to psychological and behavioral procedures. Among the disorders considered are the commonplace, for example, anxiety, depression, and alcohol abuse, as well as less frequently encountered conditions such as panic disorder in children and Munchausen syndrome. In all some 60 disorders are discussed.

Chronological coverage is broad. The main section focuses on reviews published in the last two decades while Appendix 1 brings together seminal research back to the 1950s. Appendices on cost-effectiveness and the relationship between therapy duration and outcome are also included. The conclusions and recommendations of reviewers are integrated in a series of Summary Tables. These tables highlight research-based treatment guidelines, highly versus marginally effective procedures, length-of-treatment data, and evaluations of group versus individual, and drug versus nondrug approaches. Finally, a sample of citations to recently published positive trials is provided to give the reader direct access to at least one successful outcome for each treatment and disorder.

SELECTION CRITERIA

Reviews were identified through database searches and direct inspection of the leading journals in mental health and substance abuse. They are divided into two categories. "Major Research Reviews in Core Journals" are reviews that focus exclusively on the evaluation of a particular treatment and were published in one of the top three journals in clinical psychology or one of the top ten journals in psychiatry, social work, or substance abuse. Based on citation analyses in the *Science Citation Index* and the *Social Sciences Citation Index*, these particular rankings were selected to achieve a degree of balance among the disciplines. Reviews from core journals that address but do not focus on treatment evaluation, and reviews from other respected but lower ranking journals, are discussed under "Other Significant Reviews."

SAMPLE ENTRY

Major Research Reviews in Core Journals

Scogin, F. & McElreath, L. (1994). Efficacy of psychosocial treatments for geriatric depression: A quantitative review. *Journal of Consulting and Clinical Psychology, 62,* 69-74. (rank = 1) ❶   ❷
Scogin and McElreath perform a meta-analysis on studies of a variety of psychotherapeutic procedures for the elderly. These include cognitive and behavioral techniques, and a treatment termed "reminiscence therapy" which focuses on a life review process. Patients with both clinical and subclinical levels of depression were involved. Results indicate that the various psychotherapies consistently outperformed control conditions and that group and individual methods obtained equivalent outcomes. The authors challenge the lukewarm endorsement of psychosocial interventions for geriatric depression by the National Institutes of Health and conclude that these procedures appeared to be "quite effective" with elderly patients.
Sessions < 12 ❸   Effect size = .8 ❹   15+ studies. ❺

❶   Shows journal rank based on citation analyses in the *Science Citation Index* and the *Social Sciences Citation Index.* A journal's rank reflects its standing relative to other journals in the same discipline (i.e., clinical psychology, psychiatry, social work, etc.).

❷   Full summaries are provided for "Major Research Reviews in Core Journals." Brief summaries are provided for "Other Significant Reviews."

❸   Indicates an average treatment duration of fewer than 12 sessions in the reviewed studies.

❹   Effect size is a quantitative measure calculated by the authors of most meta-analyses to indicate the relative effectiveness of a particular treatment. See Tables 1 and 2 for additional explanation.

❺   Shows the number of studies covered in a review. A "+" is used to indicate an approximation if the author of the review failed to specify the precise number of studies considered.

REVIEWS AND POSITIVE TRIALS

ALCOHOL ABUSE

Major Research Reviews in Core Journals

Agosti, V. (1994). The efficacy of controlled trials of alcohol misuse treatments in maintaining abstinence: A meta-analysis. *International Journal of the Addictions, 29,* 759-769. (rank = 8)
Agosti's meta-analysis covers reports on hospital-based, outpatient, individual, and group procedures. Care was provided by both paraprofessionals and certified counselors. Using a meta-analytic technique based on odds of success rather than effect size, the author concludes that in only 3 of 15 trials were treated patients at least twice as likely as untreated patients to be abstinent at 6- and 12-month follow-up. 15 studies.

...four studies... failed to find abstinence outcome differences when inpatient treatment was compared to outpatient treatment.

Agosti (p. 767)

Moskowitz, J.M. (1989). The primary prevention of alcohol problems: A critical review of the research literature. *Journal of Studies on Alcohol, 50,* 54-88. (rank = 2)
Moskowitz reviews empirical research and policy implications in several areas of prevention. These include drinking age, law enforcement policies, automobile safety, and prevention programs in schools, community, and the media. A host of large-scale controlled and quasi-experimental studies are reviewed. The author interprets the empirical evidence for educational programs as less promising than findings on

drinking age, alcohol taxation, and law enforcement in reducing alcohol-related problems. Supported by a grant from the National Institute on Alcohol Abuse and Alcoholism. 100+ studies.

...intervening at the marital/ family level with nonalcoholic family members can motivate an initial commitment to change in the alcoholic who is unwilling to seek help.

O'Farrell (p. 23)

O'Farrell, T.J. (1989). Marital and family therapy in alcoholism treatment. *Journal of Substance Abuse Treatment, 6,* 23-29. (rank = 6)
This review highlights mostly controlled behavioral treatment studies. Typical treatment goals included teaching the spouse how to promote the alcoholic's entry into therapy and to reinforce adherence to disulfiram and other treatment regimens. O'Farrell concludes that marital and family methods appeared to reduce drinking in the 6-month period following the start of treatment and helped stabilize marriage and family relationships. He also notes that better results were obtained when these procedures were administered in couples groups or with individual couples than when applied on a concurrent basis with the nonalcoholic spouse. 10+ studies.

Meyer, R., & Kranzler, H. (1988). Alcoholism: Clinical implications of recent research. *Journal of Clinical Psychiatry, 49(9, suppl),* 8-12. (rank = 5)
Meyer and Kranzler focus on prognostic indicators identified in the alcoholism treatment literature. Outcome data suggested that severely dependent alcoholics generally did particularly poorly in controlled drinking programs. The pres-

ence of psychopathology such as antisocial personality disorder or drug dependence was also associated with poorer outcomes. In contrast women with depression showed a better treatment response than nondepressed male counterparts in two reports. Supported by a grant from the National Institute on Alcohol Abuse and Alcoholism. 20+ studies.

Nathan, P.E., & Skinstad, A.H. (1987). Outcomes of treatment for alcohol problems: Current methods, problems, and results. *Journal of Consulting and Clinical Psychology, 55,* 332-340. (rank = 1)
In this overview Nathan and Skinstad integrate the findings of several comprehensive reviews and treatment studies from the 1970s and early 1980s. One of these reviews evaluated more than 500 outcome reports, a multicenter project involving 14,000 patients, and a 40-year longitudinal investigation. Based on their analysis, the authors raise questions concerning the lasting effectiveness of inpatient and other intensive therapies, as well as the utility of alcoholism treatment programs in general. Partially supported by a grant from the National Institute on Alcohol Abuse and Alcoholism. 20+ studies.

While tricyclic antidepressants are among the most frequently prescribed drugs for alcoholic patients, there is scant evidence for the efficacy of these drugs, even among primary depressives with alcoholism.

Meyer & Kranzler (p. 10)

Other Significant Reviews

Jarvis, T.J. (1992). Implications of gender for alcohol treatment research: A quantitative and qual-

itative review. *British Journal of Addiction, 87,* 1249-1261. (rank = 1)
Reviews comparative investigations. Notes few outcome differences between men and women. Group treatment possibly more effective with men. Funded by grant from Australian government. [See also Duckert (1987) below.]
20+ studies.

Because of the routine necessity of hospitalization and direct physician involvement, chemical aversion therapy fares very poorly in terms of cost-effectiveness.

Wilson (p. 515)

Elkins, R. (1991) An appraisal of chemical aversion (emetic therapy) approaches to alcoholism treatment. *Behaviour Research and Therapy, 29,* 387-413. (rank = 9)

Elkins, R. (1991) Chemical aversion (emetic therapy) treatment of alcoholism: Further comments. *Behaviour Research and Therapy, 29,* 421-428. (rank = 9)

Wilson, G.T. (1987). Chemical aversion conditioning as a treatment for alcoholism: A re-analysis. *Behaviour Research and Therapy, 25,* 503-516. (rank = 9)

Wilson, G. T. (1991). Chemical aversion conditioning in the treatment of alcoholism: Further comments. *Behaviour Research and Therapy, 29,* 415-419. (rank = 9)
These four reports constitute a debate in which Elkins advocates expanded availability of emetic

therapy based on laboratory research, clinical trials, and the experience of more than 35,000 alcoholics who have received treatment worldwide. Wilson argues that emetic therapy is more expensive than less intrusive forms of treatment yet not demonstrably more effective. The reviews of both authors were partially supported by funding from the National Institute on Alcohol Abuse and Alcoholism. 100+ studies.

Castaneda, R., & Cushman, P. (1989). Alcohol withdrawal: A review of clinical management. *Journal of Clinical Psychiatry, 50,* **278-284. (rank = 5)**
Emphasizes pharmacological management of withdrawal phase. Cites support for benzodiazepines, beta-blockers. Notes 90% success rate in hospital study using psychological care alone. 30+ studies.

Duckert, F. (1987). Recruitment into treatment and effects of treatment for female problem drinkers. *Addictive Behavior, 12,* **137-150. (rank = 3)**
Summarizes research on mixed-sex and all-female treatment programs. Like Jarvis (1992) above generally finds no outcome difference by gender. 10+ studies.

Traditionally there has been a widespread belief that ...women have been more difficult to treat than men, and therefore have a poorer treatment prognosis...

Duckert (p. 140)

Selected Positive Trial

Chapman, P.L.H., & Huygens, I. (1988). An evaluation of three treatment programmes for alcoholism: An experimental study with 6- and 8-month follow-ups. British Journal of Addiction, 83, 67-81. (rank = 1)

...cognitive-behavioral therapy has moved closer to psychodynamic therapy in its goals. These similarities appear to make CBT more acceptable to psychodynamically oriented practitioners than behavior therapy.

Chambless & Gillis (p. 258)

ANXIETY DISORDERS
(see also Social Phobia)

Major Research Reviews in Core Journals

Chambless, D.L., & Gillis, M.M. (1993). Cognitive therapy of anxiety disorders. Journal of Consulting and Clinical Psychology, 61, 248-260. (rank = 1)
Chambless and Gillis provide a meta-analytic review of treatment research on generalized anxiety disorder, panic disorder with and without agoraphobia, and social phobias. The authors conclude that the evidence consistently supported the superiority of cognitive procedures to waiting-list, placebo, and other control conditions, and to general supportive therapy. They also cite evidence on the limitations of combining cognitive and other psychological treatments in brief therapy. Supported by a grant from the National Institute of Mental Health. Effect size = 1.7 20+ studies.

Berman, J.S., Miller, R.C., & Massman, P.J. (1985). Cognitive therapy versus systematic desensitization: Is one treatment superior? *Psychological Bulletin, 97,* 451-461. (rank = 3)

This review considers studies which directly compared cognitive and desensitization procedures. Most trials involved brief therapy for anxiety disorders. Using meta-analytic techniques, the authors find both procedures superior to no-treatment controls and approximately equal in effectiveness. The combination of cognitive therapy and desensitization also proved superior to no treatment but offered no significant advantage over either therapy administered singly. Sessions < 12 25 studies.

Our review also reveals that therapies combining both cognitive and desensitization treatments are no more effective than one of the treatments alone.

Berman et al (p. 451)

Delmonte, M.M. (1985). Meditation and anxiety reduction: A literature review. *Clinical Psychology Review, 5,* 91-102. (rank = 3)

Delmonte reviews mostly nonclinical studies, although trials with patient populations are also included. In four particularly well-designed trials meditation yielded significant reductions in anxiety. Moreover, the procedure proved roughly as effective as systematic desensitization, self-hypnosis, and EMG biofeedback. 20+ studies.

Other Significant Reviews

The adult anxiety syndromes that affect adolescents include panic disorder with and without agoraphobia, social phobia, generalized anxiety disorder, obsessive-compulsive disorder, and posttraumatic stress disorder...

Biederman (p.20)

Reiter, S., Kutcher, S., & Gardner, D. (1992). Anxiety disorders in children and adolescents: Clinical and related issues in pharmacological treatment. *Canadian Journal of Psychiatry, 37,* 432-438. (rank = 28)

Reviews treatment research on benzodiazepines, tricyclics. Discusses side effects, adolescent abuse, integration with family therapy, behavioral procedures. 10+ studies.

Biederman, J. (1990). The diagnosis and treatment of adolescent anxiety disorders. *Journal of Clinical Psychiatry, 51(5,suppl),* 20-26. (rank = 5)

Cites drug studies only, most with school phobia. Includes succinct guidelines for medication management. 20+ studies.

Hayward, P., Wardle, J., & Higgitt, A. (1989). Benzodiazepine research: Current findings and practical consequences. *British Journal of Clinical Psychology, 28,* 307-327. (rank = 29)

Discusses physiology, use patterns, dependence, withdrawal. Reviews effectiveness studies of psychotherapy, behavioral withdrawal strategies. 50+ studies.

Selected Positive Trial

Barlow, D.H., Rapee, R.M., & Brown, T.A. (1992). Behavioral treatment of generalized anxiety disorder. *Behavior Therapy, 23,* 551-570. (rank = 7)

ARTHRITIS

Major Research Reviews in Core Journals

Young, L.D. (1992). Psychological factors in rheumatoid arthritis. *Journal of Consulting and Clinical Psychology, 60,* 619-627. (rank = 1)
Young presents an overview of research on psychological and behavioral aspects of rheumatoid arthritis, including a brief review of treatment studies. In several trials biofeedback-assisted relaxation, stress management, and cognitive-behavioral interventions were tested against control procedures. The author concludes that cognitive-behavioral methods consistently yielded reductions in self-reported pain. These were accompanied by improvement on objective measures of disease activity in some cases.
Sessions < 12 8 studies.

Selected Positive Trial

Parker, J.C., Frank, R.G., Beck, N.C., Smarr, L.K.L. et al (1988). Pain management in rheumatoid arthritis

The concept of an "arthritic personality" has been abandoned as a consequence of the lack of supporting evidence.

Young (p. 621)

patients: A cognitive-behavioral approach. *Arthritis and Rheumatism, 31,* 593-601. (rank = 1)

ASTHMA

Psychoeducational approaches now being standardized in a national program are cost-effective.

Lehrer et al (p. 639)

Major Research Reviews in Core Journals

Lehrer, P.M., Sargunaraj, D., & Hochron, S. (1992). Psychological approaches to the treatment of asthma. *Journal of Consulting and Clinical Psychology, 60,* 639-643. (rank = 1)
Behaviorally oriented procedures are reviewed, including psychoeducational groups, relaxation training, biofeedback, and family therapy. Although few well-controlled trials were reported, the authors note that psychoeducational and relaxation techniques produced promising results as adjuncts to medical treatment. Supported by grants from the National Institutes of Health. 10+ studies.

Selected Positive Trial

Vazquez, M.I., & Buceta, J.M. (1993). Effectiveness of self-management programmes and relaxation training in the treatment of bronchial asthma: Relationships with trait anxiety and emotional attack triggers. *Journal of Psychosomatic Research, 37,* 71-81. (rank = 16)

ATTENTION-DEFICIT HYPERACTIVITY DISORDER

Major Research Reviews in Core Journals

Dulcan, M. K. (1986). Comprehensive treatment of children and adolescents with attention-deficit disorders: The state of the art. *Clinical Psychology Review, 6,* **539-569. (rank = 3)**
Dulcan's broad survey includes a review of studies that assessed drug, drug versus behavioral, and drug plus behavioral treatment. In direct comparisons drugs produced somewhat larger gains and were accompanied by higher rates of compliance. Investigations of combination treatments obtained mixed results, with the addition of behavioral techniques to drug therapy leading to enhanced effects in about half the reports considered. Partially supported by a grant from the National Institute of Mental Health.
20+ studies.

Although the combination of cognitive therapy with stimulant medication ... has considerable intuitive appeal, two recent studies have yielded discouraging results.

Dulcan (p. 562)

Abikoff, H. (1985). Efficacy of cognitive training interventions in hyperactive children: A critical review. *Clinical Psychology Review, 5,* **479-512. (rank = 3)**
Cognitive interventions for hyperactivity include self-instruction training, cognitive modeling, and behavior modification aimed at improving self-regulation skills. This report reviews studies in which outcome was primarily measured in terms

of cognitive performance, academic achievement, or school behavior. Findings were positive with regard to improvement in planning and perceptual-motor tasks. Significant gains in reading comprehension and in reducing disruptive classroom and playground behavior were also obtained in a few studies. By and large, however, Abikoff considers results with cognitive methods disappointing. Partially supported by a grant from the National Institute of Mental Health.
Sessions < 12   23 studies.

During self-instruction training, children are taught to ask and then answer a series of questions that guide them systematically through the task at hand.

Other Significant Reviews

Baer & Nietzel (p. 401)

Baer, R.A., & Nietzel, M.T. (1991). Cognitive and behavioral treatment of impulsivity in children: Meta-analytic review of the outcome literature. *Journal of Clinical Child Psychology, 20,* 400-412. (rank = 8)
Cites modest improvement in impulsivity related to attention-deficit hyperactivity disorder, conduct disorder, learning disability. Subclinical populations used in many studies. Sessions < 12   Effect size = .8   36 studies.

Lubar, J. F. (1991). Discourse on the development of EEG diagnostics and biofeedback for attention-deficit/hyperactivity disorders. *Biofeedback and Self-Regulation, 16,* 201-225. (rank = 33)
Discusses mostly author's own work, case reports, some controlled research. Highlights positive findings, treatment protocols, cost considerations. 5+ studies.

Gadow, K. (1985). Relative efficacy of pharmacological, behavioral, and combination treatments for enhancing academic performance. *Clinical Psychology Review, 5,* 513-533. (rank = 3)
Notes behavior therapy added to stimulant drug treatment enhanced academic performance of hyperactive, learning disabled children in some trials. 16 studies.

Selected Positive Trial

Carlson, C.L., Pelham, W.E., Milich, R., & Dixon, J. (1992). Single and combined effects of methylphenidate and behavior therapy on the classroom performance of children with attention-deficit hyperactivity disorder. *Journal of Abnormal Child Psychology, 20,* 213-232. (rank = 12)

A small, but not negligible, minority of people with autism lead productive, self-supporting adult lives...

Gillberg (p. 375)

AUTISM

Major Research Reviews in Core Journals - none

Other Significant Reviews

Gillberg, C. (1991). Outcome in autism and autistic-like conditions. *Journal of the American Academy of Child and Adolescent Psychiatry, 30,* 375-382. (rank = 7)
Focuses on long-term follow-up investigations of untreated children. Reports 5% of sufferers "out-

grew" condition, most remained severely handicapped. 20+ studies.

Selected Positive Trial

Intervention with low distress subjects who did not meet diagnostic criteria for outpatient-level psychiatric disturbances ... did not appear to be beneficial.

Windholz et al (p. 445)

Szatmari, P., Bartolucci, G., Brenner, R., Bond, S. et al (1989). A follow-study of high-functioning autistic children. *Journal of Autism and Developmental Disorders, 19,* **213-225. (rank = 19)**

BEREAVEMENT

Major Research Reviews in Core Journals

Windholz, M.J., Marmar, C.R., & Horowitz, M.J. (1985). A review of the research on conjugal bereavement: Impact on health and efficacy of intervention. *Comprehensive Psychiatry, 26,* **433-447. (rank = 10)**

This paper surveys research on the effects of the death of a spouse. Topics include survivor mortality, emotional and physical morbidity, and the effectiveness of psychological services during bereavement. The authors summarize evidence showing increased mortality in recent widowers, and significantly higher levels of psychological and general health problems, in both men and women, following the death of a spouse. For 20% of this population physical and psychological distress continued for as long as several years after the loss. Details are presented of controlled outcome studies of self-help and other forms of brief therapy. Treatment targeted at high risk subjects – those with poor social support or concurrent life crises – was generally most effective. 10+ studies.

Selected Positive Trial

Stroebe, M., & Stroebe, W. (1991). Does "grief work" work? *Journal of Consulting and Clinical Psychology, 59,* 479-482. (rank = 1)

Reliance on group support alone may be insufficient to produce any measurable benefit.

Andersen (p. 562)

CANCER

Major Research Reviews in Core Journals

Andersen, B.L. (1992). Psychological interventions for cancer patients to enhance the quality of life. *Journal of Consulting and Clinical Psychology, 60,* 552-568. (rank =1)
Andersen focuses on psychological methods used to improve the emotional adjustment of cancer patients. He considers only treatment studies based on experimental or quasi-experimental designs. Analysis of findings indicates that significant treatment effects were obtained by most investigators, with two studies noting biological as well as self-report indications of improvement. The author points to positive outcomes with high

risk patients as particulary noteworthy, given their increasing pain and disability in the terminal stages of the disease. [See Telch & Telch (1985) below for early research on coping interventions and Carey & Burish (1988) for treatment of chemotherapy side effects.]

... it appears that the psychological symptoms that occur during cancer chemotherapy, particularly the nausea and vomiting that occur prior to drug infusion, are acquired through an associative learning process.

Carey & Burish (p. 310)

Sessions < 12 20+ studies.

Carey, M.P., & Burish, T.G. (1988). Etiology and treatment of the psychological side effects associated with cancer chemotherapy: A critical review and discussion. *Psychological Bulletin, 104,* **307-325. (rank = 3)**

This paper evaluates controlled research on psychophysiological procedures for stress-related side effects of chemotherapy. Nausea and dysphoria were the chief complaints. The interventions tested included hypnosis, relaxation training with guided imagery, and biofeedback. All were brief, typically from three to five sessions. The authors conclude that outcome data supported the effectiveness of hypnosis, relaxation training with imagery, and desensitization. Studies on biofeedback and distraction techniques are considered inconclusive because of the use of small samples. Partially supported by grants from the National Cancer Institute and the American Cancer Society. Sessions < 12 20 studies.

Telch, C.F., & Telch, M.J. (1985). Psychological ap-

proaches for enhancing coping among cancer patients: A review. *Clinical Psychology Review, 5,* 325-344. (rank = 3)

A handful of reports dealing with support groups, patient education, and coping skills training are reviewed. All made comparisons with a no-treatment or other control condition and used quality of life indicators to gauge success. Findings, by and large, were lukewarm, with immediate gains frequently disappearing within a few months. The authors note that one study of a problem-solving procedure yielded positive results which were maintained at 6-month follow-up despite a treatment duration of only four sessions. Supported by a grant from the American Cancer Society. Sessions < 12   30+ studies.

... very brief interventions such as increased in-hospital contact show [only] minimal gains.

Wekerle & Wolfe (p. 519)

Selected Positive Trial

Burish, T.G., Carey, M.P., Krozely, M.G., & Greco, F.A. (1987). Conditioned nausea and vomiting induced by cancer chemotherapy: Prevention through behavioral treatment. *Journal of Consulting and Clinical Psychology, 55,* 42-48. (rank = 1)

CHILD ABUSE (see also Sexual Abuse)

Major Research Reviews in Core Journals

Wekerle, C., & Wolfe, D. (1993). Prevention of child

physical abuse and neglect: Promising new directions. *Clinical Psychology Review, 13,* 501-540. (rank = 3)

Most of the interventions considered in this review relied on a home visit approach. The aim was to enhance childrearing skills of teenaged mothers and others at risk for committing child abuse or neglect. In most studies home visits ranging from weekly to monthly, for 1-3 years, were compared to no treatment. Wekerle and Wolfe conclude that parental attitudes, adjustment, and childrearing skills significantly improved across studies. However, the authors note a paucity of data on long-term benefits as well as on the impact of this type of intervention on actual maltreatment of children. Partially supported by grants from the Canadian government. 34 studies.

Behaviorally-based treatment services for abuse parents typically involve ... child management skills, anger control skills, and/or general stress management.

Wolfe & Wekerle (p. 488)

Wolfe, D., & Wekerle, C. (1993). Treatment strategies for child physical abuse and neglect: A critical progress report. *Clinical Psychology Review, 13,* 473-500. (rank = 3)

This paper complements the preceding review with an emphasis on treatment rather than prevention. Three types of service are considered: child-focused therapeutic day care; parent-focused behavioral and cognitive-behavioral procedures; and multiservice programs which combined parent training and direct service components such as crisis intervention. Based on their analysis of outcome data, Wolfe and We-kerle conclude that behavioral and cognitive-behavioral procedures for improving parent coping and childrearing skills were most promising. Partially supported under contract with the Department of Health and Human Services. 21 studies.

Other Significant Reviews

MacMillan, H.L., MacMillan, J.H., Offord, D.R., Griffith, L. et al (1994). Primary prevention of child physical abuse and neglect: A critical review. Part I. *Journal of Child Psychology and Psychiatry and Allied Disciplines, 35,* 835-856. (rank = 8)
In contrast to Wekerle and Wolfe (1993) above, covers only prospective controlled trials, most with nurse home visits, high risk children. Concludes some perinatal visitation programs effective in reducing abuse, neglect. Partially supported by grant from Canadian government. 11 studies.

Selected Positive Trial

Wolf, D.A., Edwards, B., Manion, I., & Koverola, C. (1988). Early intervention for parents at risk of child abuse and neglect: A preliminary investigation. *Journal of Consulting and Clinical Psychology, 56,* 40-47. (rank = 1)

For the group receiving home visitation throughout infancy, infants presented to the emergency room fewer times in the first ...and second years of life...

MacMillan et al (p. 840)

CHILD THERAPY

Major Research Reviews in Core Journals

...cognitive-behavioral therapy should actively intervene with key individuals in the child's social environment (parents, teacher, and, possibly peers) to maintain therapeutic change.

Kendall (p. 243)

Kendall, P. (1993). Cognitive-behavioral therapies with youth: Guiding theory, current status, and emerging developments. *Journal of Consulting and Clinical Psychology, 61,* 235-247. (rank = 1)
Kendall concisely summarizes outcome research on a variety of disorders. He interprets evidence for cognitive-behavioral treatment of conduct disorders and aggression as especially encouraging but finds insufficient evidence for conclusions about anxiety, attention-deficit disorder and depression. Partially supported by a grant from the National Institute of Mental Health. 50+ studies.

Barrnett, R.J., Docherty, J.P., & Frommelt, G.M. (1991). A review of child psychotherapy research since 1963. *Journal of the American Academy of Child and Adolescent Psychiatry, 30,* 1-14. (rank = 7)
This paper presents a comprehensive review of nonbehavioral child psychotherapy, including a historical survey of previous reviews back to the 1950s. Using a "box score" approach, the authors summarize outcomes and limitations of the literature. They conclude that the generally poor quality of the studies examined makes it difficult to offer any overall judgment as to the effectiveness of nonbehavioral procedures with children. 43 studies.

Kazdin, A. (1991). Effectiveness of psychotherapy with children and adolescents. *Journal of Consulting and Clinical Psychology, 59,* 785-798. (rank = 1)

Kazdin highlights previous reviews, theoretical and research issues, and important outcome studies. He finds the various forms of therapy to be more effective than no treatment and comparable in magnitude to that of adult psychotherapy. Behavioral techniques arguably, though not conclusively, outperformed nonbehavioral methods by a slight margin. The author notes particular promise in problem-solving and parent management training for conduct problems. Partially supported by grants from the National Institute of Mental Health and the Robert Wood Johnson Foundation. [For comprehensive quantitative reviews see the meta-analyses by Weisz et al (1987) and Casey & Herman (1985) below.] 150+ studies.

Many clinical problems run in families ... for example, parents of children with anxiety disorders ... have a higher rate of anxiety disorders themselves.

Kazdin (p. 792)

Weisz, J., Weiss, B., Alicke, M., & Klotz, M. (1987). Effectiveness of psychotherapy with children and adolescents: A meta-analysis for clinicians. *Journal of Consulting and Clinical Psychology, 55,* 542-549. (rank = 1)

This wide-ranging review covers controlled studies of behavioral, nondirective, and psychodynamic methods. Anxiety, impulse disorders, and social withdrawal were the major target problems. For this broad literature as a whole, the authors conclude that: 1) the effects of the various therapies significantly exceeded the effects of control conditions and were comparable to results obtained with adults; 2) behavioral treatments outperformed nonbehavioral; and 3) no significant outcome differences were observed between individual and group techniques. A list of cited studies is not included but can be obtained from the authors. Partially supported by grants from the North Carolina Division of Mental Health, Mental Retardation and Substance Abuse Services, and the National Institute of Mental Health. Effect size = .8 108 studies.

When parents were treated, outcomes for their children... were similar to outcomes produced when treatment was administered only to the children...

Casey & Berman (p. 392)

Casey, R., & Berman, J. (1985). The outcome of psychotherapy with children. *Psychological Bulletin, 98,* 388-400. (rank = 3)

Casey and Berman also present an extensive meta-analysis across a wide range of disorders and treatments. Behavioral procedures were used in half the studies followed in frequency by client-centered and dynamic methods. Treatment was shortterm, averaging approximately 10 sessions. Their analysis indicates that the various therapies produced significantly higher rates of improvement than no treatment or placebo procedures. While behavioral methods proved superior to others, the authors note that this finding may be partially attributed to the particular outcome measures and target problems selected by researchers favoring this approach. No difference in effectiveness was observed between individual and group methods. Sessions < 12 Effect size = .7 76 studies.

Other Significant Reviews

Shirk, S.R., & Russell, R.L. (1992). A re-evaluation of estimates of child therapy effectiveness. *Journal of the American Academy of Child and Adolescent Psychiatry, 31,* 703-710. (rank = 7)
Like Barrnett et al (1991) above, argues against suggested inferiority of nonbehavioral therapy on grounds that nonbehavioral methods (client-centered, psychodynamic, etc.) not yet adequately tested. 24 studies.

... boys in at-risk environments respond more dramatically to preventive interventions than do girls.

McGuire & Earls (p. 147)

McGuire, J., & Earls, F. (1991). Prevention of psychiatric disorders in early childhood. *Journal of Child Psychology and Psychiatry and Allied Disciplines, 32,* 129-153. (rank = 8)
Surveys outcome reports on educational and mental health programs. Concludes brief interventions with at-risk neonates associated with long-term developmental gains. Supported by grant from National Institute of Justice.
Sessions < 12 30+ studies.

Selected Positive Trial

Kendall, P. C. (1994). Treating anxiety disorders in children: Results of a randomized clinical trial. *Journal of Consulting and Clinical Psychology, 62,* 100-110. (rank = 1)

CHRONIC FATIGUE SYNDROME

Major Research Reviews in Core Journals - none

Other Significant Reviews

Although there may be a high coincidence of major depression in CFS, a substantial proportion of patients lack any identifiable ...psychiatric disorder...

Krupp et al (p. 403)

Krupp, L.B., Mendelson, W.B., & Friedman, R. (1991). An overview of chronic fatigue syndrome. *Journal of Clinical Psychiatry, 52,* 403-410. (rank = 5)
Broad background paper includes discussion of pharmacotherapy, behavioral treatment.
3 studies.

Selected Positive Trial

Butler, S., Chalder, T., Ron, M., & Wessely, S. (1991). Cognitive behaviour therapy in chronic fatigue syndrome. *Journal of Neurology, Neurosurgery and Psychiatry, 54,* 153-158. (rank = 7)

COGNITIVE REHABILITATION
see Head Injury

CONDUCT DISORDER (see also Child Therapy, Juvenile Delinquency)

Major Research Reviews in Core Journals

Durlak, J., Fuhrman, T., & Lampman, C. (1991). Effectiveness of cognitive-behavior therapy for maladapting children: A meta-analysis. *Psychological Bulletin, 110,* **204-214. (rank = 3)**
This meta-analysis examines treatment research on a variety of childhood behavioral problems. The most common targets were acting-out disorders, typically treated in a school setting. Results indicate that cognitive interventions produced clinically meaningful improvements well in excess of control procedures. The analysis also indicates that 11-13 year olds did significantly better than younger children, suggesting a link between cognitive development and treatment effectiveness with this type of therapy.
Sessions < 12 Effect size = .9 50+ studies.

...the gains produced ...are quite surprising given that most treated children received very brief treatment (fewer than 10 sessions)...

Durlak et al (p.210)

Dumas, J. (1989). Treating antisocial behavior in children: Child and family approaches. *Clinical Psychology Review, 9,* **197-222. (rank = 3)**
Dumas reviews studies of cognitive and social skills training for children, parent training, and family therapy. All used experimental or quasi-experimental designs. Problem behavior ranged from fighting and temper tantrums to defiance, stealing, and lying. The author concludes that

training in social and cognitive skills such as expressing complaints and perspective-taking led to shortterm reductions in antisocial behavior but that long-term clinical effectiveness has yet to be demonstrated. Partially supported by grants from the W.T. Grant Foundation and the Medical Research Council of Canada. Sessions < 12 50+ studies.

Research has indicated that a high rate of childhood aggression. even in children as young as age 3, is fairly stable over time.

Webster-Stratton (p. 1047)

Other Significant Reviews

Lochman, J., & Lenhart, L. (1993). Anger coping intervention for aggressive children: Conceptual models and outcome effects. *Clinical Psychology Review, 13,* 785-805. (rank = 3)
Finds cognitive-behavioral procedures including problem-solving training, self-instruction, moderately effective. Partially supported by grant from National Institute of Mental Health. 20+ studies.

Webster-Stratton, C. (1991). Strategies for helping families with conduct-disordered children. *Journal of Child Psychology and Psychiatry and Allied Disciplines, 32,* 1047-1062. (rank = 8)
Brief review of outcome research indicates parent training highly promising in well-designed studies, social skills training for children less encouraging. Supported by grant from National Institutes of Health. 20+ studies.

Selected Positive Trial

Kazdin, A.E., Siegel, T.C., & Bass, D. (1992). Cognitive problem-solving skills training and parent management training in the treatment of antisocial behavior in children. *Journal of Consulting and Clinical Psychology, 60,* 733-747. (rank = 1)

DEMENTIA

Major Research Reviews in Core Journals - none

Other Significant Reviews

Fisher, J., & Carstensen, L. (1990). Behavior management of the dementias. *Clinical Psychology Review, 10,* 611-629. (rank = 3)
General overview briefly discusses treatments for wandering, inappropriate sexual behavior, incontinence, eating difficulties, other dementia-related problems. Partially supported by grant from National Institute on Aging. 10+ studies.

Selected Positive Trial

Burgio, L., Engel, B.T., McCormick, K., Hawkins, A. et al (1988). Behavioral treatment for urinary incontinence in elderly inpatients: Initial attempts to modify prompting and toileting procedures. *Behavior Therapy, 19,* 345-357. (rank = 7)

...behavior problems... lead to institutionalization more often than problems directly associated with memory impairment...

Fisher & Carstensen (p. 612)

DEPRESSION – Standard Therapies

Major Research Reviews in Core Journals

On the whole, we doubt that either cognitive therapy, or pharmacotherapy, will prove to be superior to the other in the treatment of the average nonpsychotic, nonbipolar depressed outpatient.

Hollon et al (p. 272)

Hollon, S., Shelton, R., & Davis, D. (1993). Cognitive therapy for depression: Conceptual issues and clinical efficacy. *Journal of Consulting and Clinical Psychology, 61,* 270-275. (rank = 1)
Hollon et al provide a concise overview of outcome research on cognitive therapy. The paper is especially noteworthy for its detailed analysis of unsettled efficacy issues. The authors discuss the inadequacy of drug protocols in comparative trials, anomalous findings of the NIMH study in which cognitive therapy fared less well than in most other studies, the possibly underreported additive effects of cognitive therapy in combination treatments, and the potential for relapse prevention noted by some investigators. [To gain a full perspective on this extensive literature, see also the reviews by Hollon et al (1991) and Dobson (1989) below.] 30+ studies.

Robins, C., & Hayes, A. (1993). An appraisal of cognitive therapy. *Journal of Consulting and Clinical Psychology, 61,* 205-214. (rank = 1)
Robins and Hayes limit their review to the particular form of cognitive therapy developed by Beck. Citing earlier reviews and additional investigations, they conclude that most outcome data supported the equivalent effectiveness of

cognitive therapy and pharmacotherapy in the treatment of depression. In addition they discern no additive effect in the combination of cognitive procedures and drug therapy for depression. Findings regarding other conditions are considered more tentative. 10+ studies.

Hollon, S., Shelton, R., & Loosen, P. (1991). Cognitive therapy and pharmacotherapy for depression. *Journal of Consulting and Clinical Psychology, 59,* **88-99. (rank = 1)**

Reports comparing cognitive therapy and drug treatment are reviewed from the decade following the first controlled study of cognitive therapy for depression in the late 1970s. The authors conclude that cognitive therapy and pharmacotherapy achieved comparable results with non-psychotic, nonbipolar outpatients in most of these studies although relapse rates were somewhat lower for patients who received cognitive treatment. There was no indication that the combination of the modalities offered an advantage over either administered singly. [For additional discussion of outcome research on drug versus, and combined with, psychotherapy see the preceding review by Hollon et al (1993), and Robinson et al (1990), Conte et al (1986), and Meterissian and Bradwejn (1989) below.] 50+ studies.

Robinson, L., Berman, J., & Neimeyer, R. (1990). Psychotherapy for the treatment of depression: A com-

... Beck initially investigated the thoughts and dreams of depressed individuals, looking for signs of repressed hostility. Instead, he discovered a prominent theme of defeat and a pervasive negative bias.

Robins & Hayes (p. 205)

prehensive review of controlled outcome research. *Psychological Bulletin, 108,* 30-49. (rank = 3)

Robinson et al present two meta-analyses. In one they evaluate clinical trials of cognitive, behavioral, cognitive-behavioral, and general verbal therapies which were tested against each other or a no-treatment or control condition. A second analysis considers studies that directly compared the above treatments with pharmacotherapy. Results indicate that each mode of therapy produced substantial improvement, significantly greater than that of no treatment, and that this was maintained at follow-up. No significant differences are detected among psychological treatments or between psychotherapy and drug treatment, nor is the combination of pharmacotherapy and psychotherapy found to be superior to either administered singly. Findings of the meta-analysis also support the equivalence of group and individual formats and the absence of a significant correlation between length of treatment and outcome. Sessions < 12 Effect size = .7 58 studies, analysis 1; 15 studies, analysis 2.

... results ...are equivalent with respect to the utility of cognitive therapy for the elderly ...

Dobson
(p. 418)

Dobson, K. (1989). A meta-analysis of the efficacy of cognitive therapy for depression. *Journal of Consulting and Clinical Psychology, 57,* 414-419. (rank = 1)

This report focuses exclusively on studies which made reference to the procedures developed by Beck and used the Beck Depression Inventory as an outcome measure. Trials are included which compared cognitive therapy to an alternative procedure, no treatment, or a wait-list control. Dobson concludes that patients, on average, reported reliably larger gains with cognitive therapy than with either behavior therapy, drug therapy, or any of the other conditions tested. He observes no correlation between length of treatment and outcome. Sessions < 12   Effect size = 2.2   28 studies.

Nietzel, M., Russell, R., Hemmings, K., & Gretter, M. (1987). Clinical significance of psychotherapy for unipolar depression: A meta-analytic approach to social comparison. *Journal of Consulting and Clinical Psychology, 55,* 156-161. (rank = 1)
Nietzel et al seek to determine whether the statistically significant effects obtained in psychotherapy studies were also clinically significant. To do this they examine a large number of treatment studies, most cognitive and/or behavioral, to assess how posttreatment depression levels of patients compared with those of the general population. The authors conclude that the results of treatment were moderately significant in clinical terms. That is, the average patient progressed from a pre-treatment depression level above the 99th percentile of the general population to approximately the 74th percentile at 4-month follow-up. Individual treatment was associated with greater gains than group methods, while no relationship was found between treatment duration and results. 31 studies.

Are clinically significant outcomes maintained at follow-up? Our answer is a rather confident "yes."

Nietzel et al (p. 160)

Conte, H.R., Plutchik, R., Wild, K.V., & Karasu, T.B. (1986). Combined psychotherapy and pharmacotherapy for depression. A systematic analysis of the evidence. *Archives of General Psychiatry, 43,* 471-479. (rank = 1)

The combination of psychotherapy and pharmacotherapy is probably the most commonly prescribed treatment for depression.

Conte et al (p. 471)

This paper reviews controlled studies that compared the effectiveness of psychotherapy plus drug therapy to either treatment administered alone. The authors use a novel meta-analytic technique which places strong emphasis on the quality of the reviewed studies. Various forms of psychotherapy are considered including marital, interpersonal, cognitive, and behavioral. Conte et al's analysis indicates that the combination of treatments was appreciably more effective than placebo or minimum contact conditions and slightly, but consistently, superior to psychotherapy or drug therapy alone in the treatment of depression. Sessions < 12 17 studies.

Other Significant Reviews

Meterissian, G., & Bradwejn, J. (1989). Comparative studies on the efficacy of psychotherapy, pharmacotherapy, and their combination in depression: Was adequate pharmacotherapy provided? *Journal of Clinical Psychopharmacology, 9,* 334-339. (rank = 4)

Briefly summarizes comparative trials. Concludes use of non-optimal drug protocol in some

studies may have clouded results. [See Hollon et al (1993), Hollon et al (1991), Robinson et al (1990), and Conte et al (1986) above for additional discussion of combination therapies.]
11 studies.

Paykel, E. (1989). Treatment of depression: The relevance of research for clinical practice. *British Journal of Psychiatry, 155,* 754-763. (rank = 6)
Concise summary of strengths, weaknesses of clinical findings on electroconvulsive therapy, drug treatment, psychotherapy. 30+ studies.

Selected Positive Trial

Shapiro, D.A., Barkham, M., Rees, A., Hardy, G.E. et al (1994). Effects of treatment duration and severity of depression on the effectiveness of cognitive-behavioral and psychodynamic-interpersonal psychotherapy. *Journal of Consulting and Clinical Psychology, 62,* 522-534. (rank = 1)

Cognitive therapy is... a child of the 1970s: verbal, exciting, a little pushy, perhaps riding for a fall.

Paykel
(p. 759)

DEPRESSION – Special Therapies

Major Research Reviews in Core Journals

Sleep deprivation is an attractive antidepressant treatment because it acts rapidly and is noninvasive, inexpensive, and well tolerated by most patients.

*Leibenluft & Wehr
(p. 159)*

Weissman, M.M., & Markowitz, J.C. (1994). Interpersonal psychotherapy: Current status. *Archives of General Psychiatry, 51,* 599-606. (rank = 1)
This paper describes treatment procedures and reviews research on interpersonal psychotherapy, a time-limited treatment developed for depression but now extended to other disorders as well. The majority of studies targeted depression. Other conditions included HIV-related distress, substance abuse, and bulimia. According to the authors, outcome data lent preliminary support to the usefulness of interpersonal psychotherapy for major depression. A brief summary of clinical practice guidelines for depression issued by the Department of Health and Human Services is included. 15+ studies.

Leibenluft, E., & Wehr T. (1992). Is sleep deprivation useful in the treatment of depression? *American Journal of Psychiatry, 149,* 159-168. (rank =2)
Leibenluft and Wehr review clinical studies which tested whether sleep deprivation can potentiate, hasten, or help predict responsiveness to antidepressant medication. Typically, the patient remained awake for 36 hours, one to two times per week, with this procedure. According to the authors, results were promising with respect to

hastening the onset and enhancing the overall effectiveness of antidepressant drugs. They note, however, an absence of controlled designs in much of this literature. 38 studies.

Simons, A., Epstein, L., McGowan, C., & Kupfer, D. (1985). Exercise as a treatment for depression: An update. *Clinical Psychology Review, 5,* 553-568. (rank = 3)
The rationale for this form of therapy rests on the assumption that sustained physical exercise can produce biochemical and physiological changes that affect mood. Simons et al evaluate studies which compared running, cycling, walking, and other forms of exercise to standard psychological procedures such as brief psychotherapy, cognitive therapy, and relaxation training. They interpret results as "cautiously optimistic," supporting at least the shortterm efficacy of exercise programs with clinical populations. Partially supported by a grant from the National Institute of Mental Health. Sessions < 12 7 studies.

... another framework to explain exercise effects
...maintains that treatments are effective because they restore a sense of self-efficacy...

Simons et al (p. 563)

Other Significant Reviews

Blehar, M.C., & Lewy, A.J. (1990). Seasonal mood disorders: Consensus and controversy. *Psychopharmacology Bulletin, 26,* 465-494. (rank = 17)
Comprehensive survey covers epidemiology, assessment, diagnosis, pathophysiology, treatment. Reviews studies of light therapy, drug treatment,

use of light therapy for other conditions (e.g. sleep disorders). 20+ studies.

Lam, R.W., Cripke, D.F., & Gillin, J.C. (1989). Photo-therapy for depressive disorders: A review. *Ca-nadian Journal of Psychiatry, 34,* 140-147. (rank = 28)

Although its mechanism of action remains to be explained, phototherapy appears to be a safe and effective treatment for seasonal depression...

Data from controlled studies suggested treatment safe, effective, typical response rates 60% versus 20% for placebo light conditions. Partially supported by grant from Psychiatric Research Foundation of Canada. 10+ studies.

Lam et al (p. 140)

Terman, M., Terman, J., Quitkin, F., McGrath, P. et al (1989). Light therapy for seasonal affective disorder: A review of efficacy. *Neuropsychopharmacology, 2,* 1-22. (rank = 5)

In-depth evaluation of pooled data from published, unpublished reports. Notes symptomatic improvement in mild depression. Partially supported by grants from National Institute of Mental Health. 20+ studies.

Wulsin, L., Bachop, M., & Hoffman, D. (1988). Group therapy in manic-depressive illness. *American Journal of Psychotherapy, 42,* 263-271. (rank = 43)

Cites evidence of improved outcome when long-term drug treatment combined with adjunctive group therapy. 4 studies.

Selected Positive Trial

Dessauer, M., Goetze, U., & Tolle, R. (1985). Periodic sleep deprivation in drug-refractory depression. *Neuropsychobiology, 13,* 111-116. (rank = 46)

DEPRESSION – Special Topics

Major Research Reviews in Core Journals

Markowitz, J.C. (1994). Psychotherapy of dysthymia. *American Journal of Psychiatry, 151,* 1114-1121. (rank = 2)
Dysthymia is a form of chronic depression thought to afflict 3% of the population. Markowitz provides a comprehensive overview of this disorder, with an emphasis on nonpharmacologic treatment. He reviews outcome studies of interpersonal therapy, combined approaches, and brief cognitive-behavioral treatment, the most systematically researched intervention for dysthymia. Although most studies were small-scale and uncontrolled, successes were noted and Markowitz interprets findings as hopeful. The author includes detailed treatment guidelines. Partially supported by a grant from the National Institute of Mental Health. 10+ studies.

The rationale for antidysthymic psychotherapy should be clear. Roughly one-half of dysthymic patients do not respond to antidepressant medication.

Markowitz (p. 1114)

Scogin, F., & McElreath, L. (1994). Efficacy of psychosocial treatments for geriatric depression: A quantitative review. *Journal of Consulting and Clinical Psychology, 62,* 69-74. (rank = 1)

Scogin and McElreath perform a meta-analysis on studies of a variety of psychotherapeutic procedures for the elderly. These include cognitive and behavioral techniques, and a treatment termed "reminiscence therapy" which focuses on a life review process. Patients with both clinical and subclinical levels of depression were involved. Results indicate that the various psychotherapies consistently outperformed control conditions and that group and individual methods obtained equivalent outcomes. The authors challenge the lukewarm endorsement of psychosocial interventions for geriatric depression by the National Institutes of Health and conclude that these procedures appeared to be "quite effective" with elderly patients. Sessions < 12
Effect size = .8   17 studies.

Because so few studies have compared psychosocial and pharmacologic therapies for geriatric depression, it seems premature to advocate one modality over another.

Scogin & McElreath (p. 73)

Other Significant Reviews

Piccinelli, M., & Wilkinson, G. (1994). Outcome of depression in psychiatric settings. *British Journal of Psychiatry, 164,* 297-304. (rank = 6)

Considers inpatient and outpatient follow-up studies, 3 months to 20 years. Data indicated recurrence within 1 year for 25% of patients, within 10 years for 75% of patients. 51 studies.

Howland, R.H. (1993). Chronic depression. *Hospital and Community Psychiatry, 44,* 633-639. (rank = 19)
Emphasizes drug, combination treatments. Indicates monoamine oxidase inhibitors, serotonergic antidepressants possibly more effective than tricyclics, drug treatment plus psychotherapy promising. 10+ studies.

Conte, H., & Karasu, T. (1992). A review of treatment studies of minor depression: 1980-1991. *American Journal of Psychotherapy, 46,* 58-74. (rank = 43)
Covers drug, nondrug studies. Notes some success with antidepressants, cognitive therapy, poor results with sedative hypnotic drugs. 20+ studies.

Laberge, B., Gauthier, J., Cote, G., Plamondon, J. et al (1992). The treatment of coexisting panic and depression: A review of the literature. *Journal of Anxiety Disorders, 6,* 169-180. (rank = 17)
Reviews data on prevalence, outcome for drug, nondrug treatment. Concludes cognitive-behavioral therapy moderately effective in panic disorder with secondary depression. Provides detailed clinical recommendations. Partially supported by grant from Medical Research Council of Canada. 10+ studies.

Parker, G., Roy, K., Hadzi, P.D., & Pedic, F. (1992). Psychotic (delusional) depression: A meta-analysis of physical treatments. *Journal of Affective Disorders, 24,* 17-24. (rank = 16)

Recent clinical research suggests that depressed panic patients have more severe panic symptomatology than those who do not suffer from depression.

Laberge et al (p. 169)

Evaluates controlled studies of drug, electroconvulsive therapy. Suggests both treatments effective. ECT, tricyclics plus antipsychotics superior to tricyclics alone. Supported by grant from Australian government. Effect size for ECT = 2.3 44 studies.

...a simple weekly support group for discharged elderly depressives resulted in significant reductions of relapse and readmissions over 1 year.

Baldwin (p. 398)

Baldwin, B. (1991). The outcome of depression in old age. *International Journal of Geriatric Psychiatry, 6,* 395-400. (rank = 22)
Reviews treatment research, emphasis on long-term prognosis. Finds 70-80% shortterm recovery rate, good long-term prognosis for 60% of treated patients. Discusses aftercare, prophylaxis. 5+ studies.

Belsher, G., & Costello, C.G. (1988). Relapse after recovery from unipolar depression: A critical review. *Psychological Bulletin, 104,* 84-96. (rank = 3)
Focuses on relapse studies. Concludes 50% relapse rate within 2 years. Maintenance drugs, psychotherapy somewhat effective in preventing relapse. 10+ studies.

Selected Positive Trial

Mercier, M.A., Stewart, J.W., & Quitkin, F.M. (1992). A pilot sequential study of cognitive therapy and pharmacotherapy of atypical depression. *Journal of Clinical Psychiatry, 53,* 166-170. (rank = 5)

DIABETES

Major Research Reviews in Core Journals

Cox, D., & Gonder-Frederick, L. (1992). Major developments in behavioral diabetes research. *Journal of Consulting and Clinical Psychology, 60,* **628-638. (rank = 1)**
This wide-ranging review includes a brief discussion of behavioral weight-loss trials. Pre-post reductions in blood glucose levels were found in all studies, most of which obtained follow-up data at 3 months or more. The authors conclude there was a probable modest correlation between pounds lost and improved metabolic control, that women showed increased weight loss when treated together with husbands, and that exercise and very low calorie diets can improve outcome. Partially supported by grants from the National Institutes of Health. 9 studies.

A 10-pound weight loss has been associated with improved metabolic control ...

Cox & Gonder-Frederick (p. 633)

Other Significant Reviews

Fonagy, P., & Moran, G. (1990). Studies on the efficacy of child psychoanalysis. *Journal of Consulting and Clinical Psychology, 58,* **684-695. (rank = 1)**
Reviews psychoanalytic interventions to improve children's self-management of diabetes. Discusses quantitative methods in psychoanalytic research. 3 studies.

Goodall, T, & Halford, W. (1991). Self-management of diabetes mellitus: A critical review. *Health Psychology, 10,* 1-8. (rank = 8)
Evaluates behavioral treatment studies. Notes moderate increase in self-care skills, improved shortterm control of glucose. 5+ studies.

Selected Positive Trial

Gilden, J.L., Hendryx, M.S., Clar, S., Casia, C. et al (1992). Diabetes support groups improve health care of older diabetic patients. *Journal of the American Geriatrics Society, 40,* 147-150. (rank = 1)

DIVORCE

Major Research Reviews in Core Journals

Grych, J., & Fincham, F. (1992). Interventions for children of divorce: Toward greater integration of research and action. *Psychological Bulletin, 111,* 434-454. (rank = 3)
This review covers mostly group treatment programs designed to ameliorate the effects of divorce. It does not address routine child psychotherapy or counseling for emotional and behavioral problems that may accompany divorce. Interventions included children's groups focused on social support and coping, parenting

Perhaps the most consistent finding ...is that, on average, children from divorced families exhibit higher levels of externalizing problems such as aggression and conduct disorder than children from intact families.

Grych & Fincham (p. 435)

groups, and predivorce mediation services aimed at reducing litigation and postsettlement adjustment difficulties. Grych and Fincham consider research findings inconclusive, although impressionistic support for these interventions was strong. Supported by grants from the National Institute of Mental Health and the Guggenheim and W.T. Grant Foundations. Sessions < 12 20+ studies.

...exposure and response prevention adds little or nothing to the effectiveness of cognitive-behavioral therapy.

Wilson & Fairburn (p. 266)

Selected Positive Trial

Alpert-Gillis, L.J., Pedro-Carroll, J.L., & Cowen, E.L. (1989). The children of divorce intervention program: Development, implementation, and evaluation of a program for young urban children. *Journal of Consulting and Clinical Psychology, 57,* 583-589. (rank = 1)

DRUG ABUSE see Substance Abuse

EATING DISORDERS

Major Research Reviews in Core Journals

Wilson, G., & Fairburn, C. (1993). Cognitive treatments for eating disorders. *Journal of Consulting and Clinical Psychology, 61,* 261-269. (rank = 1)

This paper presents an overview of cognitive-behavioral therapy for bulimia nervosa and a brief review of recent outcome research. Treatment typically emphasized the modification of abnormal attitudes regarding body shape and weight, and the substitution of normal eating patterns for dysfunctional dieting. According to the authors, findings of well-controlled studies supported remission rates for cognitive-behavioral therapy in the range of 50-70% for binge eating and 35-60% for purging. The cognitive approach proved more effective than antidepressants in three comparative studies but not clearly superior to other forms of psychotherapy in a half-dozen other reports. 10+ studies.

...a provocative finding based on a national sample of 628 women with eating disorders ...suggests that the shortterm prognosis for bulimia among women in their mid-20s tends toward modest "spontaneous" improvement.

Yager (p. 24)

Yager, J. (1988). The treatment of eating disorders. *Journal of Clinical Psychiatry, 49(9,suppl)*, 18-25. (rank = 5)

Yager addresses etiology, assessment, and treatment of anorexia and bulimia nervosa, including highlights of controlled and uncontrolled outcome studies. Psychological, behavioral, and drug therapies are included. The author concludes that patients did better with treatment than without and that nearly 50% of sufferers returned to within 15% of normal body weight in several well-controlled studies. No single form of therapy appeared to stand out as clearly superior. Succinct research-based treatment guidelines are presented for each disorder. 30+ studies.

Other Significant Reviews

Abbott, D.W., & Mitchell, J.E. (1993). Antidepressants versus psychotherapy in the treatment of bulimia nervosa. *Psychopharmacology Bulletin, 29,* 115-119. (rank = 17)
Examines few available comparison trials of drug, behavioral treatment. Concludes intensive behavioral treatment possibly most effective, less intensive behavior therapy plus antidepressants also effective. 3 studies.

The shortterm effect of shortterm treatments for bulimia is dependent on the therapy dose, which should not be less than about 15 sessions for any clinically relevant effect to occur.

Hartmann et al (p. 165)

Hartmann, A., Herzog, T., & Drinkmann, A. (1992). Psychotherapy of bulimia nervosa: What is effective? A meta-analysis. *Journal of Psychosomatic Research, 36,* 159-167. (rank = 16)
Reviews mostly brief cognitive-behavioral procedures, few psychodynamic reports. Finds treatment moderately to highly effective, no difference between group and individual therapy. Effect size = 1.0 18 studies.

Walsh, B.T., & Devlin, M.J. (1992). The pharmacologic treatment of eating disorders. *Psychiatric Clinics of North America, 15,* 149-160. (rank = 30)
Controlled drug studies for bulimia, anorexia nervosa evaluated. Little evidence of drug effectiveness. Recommends initial trial of psychotherapy, behavioral treatment plus pharmacotherapy for selected patients. 20+ studies.

Mitchell, J.E. (1991). A review of the controlled trials of psychotherapy for bulimia nervosa. *Journal of Psychosomatic Research, 35 (suppl 1),* 23-31. (rank = 16)

Assesses behavioral, cognitive-behavioral, psychoeducational procedures. Notes reduction rather than elimination of symptoms, individual, group equally effective. Partially supported by grants from Public Health Service. 14 studies.

In the anorexia nervosa studies, mortality ranged from 0% to 22% of patients, with over half of the studies reporting 4% or less.

Herzog et al (p. 131)

Cox, G.L., & Merkel, W.T. (1989). A qualitative review of psychosocial treatments for bulimia. *Journal of Nervous and Mental Disease, 177,* 77-84. (rank = 11)

Evaluates individual, group treatment, mostly behavioral, cognitive-behavioral, some psychodynamic. Reports follow-up remission rates near 40%, no significant differences among treatments, individual versus group, shorter versus longer duration. 32 studies.

Herzog, D.B., Keller, M.B., & Lavori, P.W. (1988). Outcome in anorexia nervosa and bulimia nervosa: A review of the literature. *Journal of Nervous and Mental Disease, 176,* 131-143. (rank = 11)

Emphasizes follow-up studies. Cites recovery rates 17-77%, relapse rates 4-9%. Tabular summaries of numerous outcome variables included. 40 studies.

Laessle, R.G., Zoettl, C., & Pirke, K. (1987). Meta-analysis of treatment studies for bulimia. *International Journal of Eating Disorders, 6,* 647-653. (rank = 14)
Covers outcome studies of drug, psychological methods. Finds considerable improvement with psychological procedures, significantly greater than with drug therapy. Dietary management plus cognitive-behavioral techniques effective. Effect size for psychotherapy plus dietary management = 1.3   Effect size for drug therapy = .6   23 studies.

Selected Positive Trial

...ECT results in remission in about 60% of manic patients who show a poor therapeutic response to lithium or neuroleptics...

Mukherjee et al (p. 174)

Mitchell, J.E., Pyle, R.L., Eckert, E.D., Hatsukami, D. et al (1990). A comparison study of antidepressants and structured intensive group psychotherapy in the treatment of bulimia nervosa. *Archives of General Psychiatry, 47,* 149-57. (rank = 1)

ELECTROCONVULSIVE THERAPY

Major Research Reviews in Core Journals

Mukherjee, S., Sackeim, H.A., & Schnur, D.B. (1994). Electroconvulsive therapy of acute manic episodes. A review of 50 years' experience. *American Journal of Psychiatry, 151,* 169-176. (rank = 2)
This paper offers a detailed assessment of out-

come, cognitive consequences, predictors of success, and procedural issues such as frequency and duration of treatment. While early reports were largely impressionistic, four controlled studies, two retrospective and two prospective, were carried out in recent years. Mukherjee et al interpret findings as highly positive, with 80% of patients experiencing complete remission or marked clinical improvement across studies. Moreover, the authors note enhanced cognitive performance as measured by standardized intelligence tests in some patients. Partially supported by a grant from the National Institute of Mental Health. Sessions < 12 15 studies.

Recent MRI studies have failed to show shortterm anatomic changes in the brain related to acute ECT treatments.

Monroe (p. 955)

Monroe, R.R. (1991). Maintenance electroconvulsive therapy. *Psychiatric Clinics of North America, 14*, 947-960. (rank = 30)
Monroe reviews mostly uncontrolled investigations of ECT for prevention of relapse and rehospitalization in chronically ill patients. Data on more than 800 persons suffering from affective disorders or organic brain syndromes are considered. Frequency of treatment ranged from weekly to monthly over a mean duration of 33 months. Results are seen as promising, especially for medication-intolerant patients and those with relapsing or psychotic depression. The author outlines treatment guidelines and risk-benefit concerns. 14 studies.

Rifkin, A. (1988). ECT versus tricyclic antidepressants in depression: A review of the evidence. *Journal of Clinical Psychiatry, 49,* 3-7. (rank = 5)
Rifkin's review focuses on controlled studies. Although findings are considered "suggestive" of the superiority of ECT, the author concludes that inadequate data analysis and drug dose in most investigations preclude a definitive verdict on the relative efficacy of the two treatments. Rifkin includes an analysis of social and economic impediments to further research. 9 studies.

Drug treatment is usualy less expensive, but this might not be true if the patient responded more reliably and quickly to ECT and returned to work sooner.

Rifkin
(p. 6)

Janicak, P., Davis, J., Gibbons, R., Ericksen, S. et al (1985). Efficacy of ECT: A meta-analysis. *American Journal of Psychiatry, 142,* 297-302. (rank = 2)
This review considers studies which compared ECT to either simulated ECT, antidepressant medication, or drug placebo. Results of the meta-analysis indicate that ECT significantly outperformed each of these alternative procedures, yielding an "efficacy rate" of nearly 80% across studies. The authors discuss the negative findings of some studies which they consider misleading due to the use of inadequate patient samples. 10 studies.

Selected Positive Trial

Buchan, H., Johnstone, E.C., McPherson, K., Palmer, R.L. et al (1992). Who benefits from electro-

convulsive therapy? Combined results of the Leicester and Northwick Park trials. *British Journal of Psychiatry, 160,* 355-359. (rank = 6)

...the evidence from this review suggests that cure rather than management is a realistic goal for the majority of children ...

Houts et al (p. 743)

ENURESIS

Major Research Reviews in Core Journals

Houts, A.C., Berman, J.S., & Abramson, H. (1994). Effectiveness of psychological and pharmacological treatments for nocturnal enuresis. *Journal of Consulting and Clinical Psychology, 62,* 737-745. (rank = 1)

This paper presents a non-meta-analytic quantitative review of controlled outcome research. Approximately half the studies tested psychological treatments, mostly alarm-based procedures, supplemented in some cases by behavior modification. Most drug trials involved tricyclic antidepressants or desmopressin. The authors conclude that findings strongly favored the alarm method, with roughly 50% of alarm-treated patients completely symptom-free at follow-up compared to less than a fifth of those receiving alternative psychological or drug interventions. The authors further note that the addition of behavior modification (e.g. dry bed training) did not appear to enhance the basic alarm procedure. A list of reviewed studies is not included but can be obtained from the authors. Partially supported by a grant from the National Institute of Mental Health. 78 studies.

Selected Positive Trial

Boggs, S.R., Geffken, G.R., Johnson, S.B., & Silverstein, J. (1992). Behavioral treatment of nocturnal enuresis in children with insulin-dependent diabetes mellitus. *Journal of Pediatric Psychology, 17,* 111-118. (rank = 15)

Once an affect-laden image is created, patients are asked to construct a statement which best summarizes their memory.

Acierno et al (p. 289)

EYE-MOVEMENT DESENSITIZATION AND REPROCESSING (EMDR)

Major Research Reviews in Core Journals

Acierno, R., Hersen, M., van Hasselt, V.B., Tremont, G. et al (1994). Review of the validation and dissemination of eye-movement desensitization and reprocessing: A scientific and ethical dilemma. *Clinical Psychology Review, 14,* 287-299. (rank = 3)
EMDR is an imagery-based procedure used to treat trauma-related anxiety. Developed in the 1980s, it has generated controversy related to alleged restrictions on therapist training and the public dissemination of procedural details. Acierno et al discuss ethical and scientific issues involved in the controversy and review the treatment literature. They conclude that results of uncontrolled studies were generally positive but

should be interpreted with caution due to a reliance on impressionistic rather than objective or standardized outcome measures. The four controlled investigations reviewed also produced some positive results. However, according to Acierno et al, findings of these particular studies did not appear to support the effectiveness of specific EMDR procedures beyond their general imagery and exposure components. The authors note that additional research using larger patient samples and objective assessment appears warranted. [For a full discussion by the originator of EMDR, published subsequent to the present review, see Shapiro, F. (1995). *Eye-movement desensitization and reprocessing: Basic principles, protocols, and procedures.* New York: Guilford.] 10+ studies.

In the last 10 years, there has been a substantial decrease in attention to behavioral aspects of peptic ulcer disease, primarily because pharmacologic treatment is very effective.

Whitehead (p. 610)

Selected Positive Trial

Jensen, J.A. (1994). An investigation of eye-movement desensitization and reprocessing (EMD/R) as a treatment for posttraumatic stress disorder (PTSD) symptoms of Vietnam combat veterans. *Behavior Therapy, 25,* 311-325. (rank = 7)

FAMILY THERAPY See Marital and Family Therapy

GASTROINTESTINAL DISORDERS

Major Research Reviews in Core Journals

Whitehead, W. (1992). Behavioral medicine approaches to gastrointestinal disorders. *Journal of Consulting and Clinical Psychology, 60,* 605-612. (rank = 1)
Whitehead presents a broad overview of psychological and behavioral factors in gastrointestinal disorders. Based on a number of well-controlled investigations, he finds stress management, relaxation training, and biofeedback particularly promising for fecal incontinence, irritable bowel syndrome, and vomiting disorders. Results were less encouraging with ulcerative colitis and Crohn's disease. Supported by a grant from the National Institute of Mental Health. 20+ studies.

Population surveys have estimated the prevalence of IBS in the general population from 8% to 17%.

Blanchard et al (p. 349)

Other Significant Reviews

Blanchard, E., Schwarz, S., & Radnitz, C. (1987). Psychological assessment and treatment of irritable bowel syndrome. *Behavior Modification, 11,* 348-372. (rank = 28)
Reviews mostly controlled research. Cites success rates exceeding 50% for relaxation training, biofeedback, individual, group formats.
Sessions < 12 10+ studies.

Selected Positive Trial

Greene, B., & Blanchard, E.B. (1994). Cognitive therapy for irritable bowel syndrome. *Journal of Consulting and Clinical Psychology, 62,* 576-582. (rank = 1)

HEAD INJURY (see also Memory Disorders)

Major Research Reviews in Core Journals

...the inconsistency of findings and the noted methodological problems greatly limit the claim that cognitive remediation is a valid treatment approach for all head-injured patients.

Benedict (p. 623)

McGlynn, S. (1990). Behavioral approaches to neuropsychological rehabilitation. *Psychological Bulletin, 108,* 420-441. (rank = 3)

McGlynn reviews behavioral treatment studies of neuropsychological disorders associated with trauma and disease. Target problems included deficits in attention, motivation, memory, language, speech, and social behavior. Token economy and other feedback and reinforcement techniques along with training in self-instruction and self-monitoring were the most common procedures. Although the majority of reports were case studies, several well-designed single-subject investigations lent added support to findings. Overall, the author notes "considerable evidence" of success, especially with regard to memory deficits and inappropriate social behavior. 30+ studies.

Benedict, R. (1989). The effectiveness of cognitive remediation strategies for victims of traumatic head injury: A review of the literature. *Clinical Psychology Review, 9,* 605-26. (rank = 3)

Benedict evaluates treatment research on trauma associated with a rapid acceleration or deceleration of the skull. Most reports were case studies or single-subject designs which used cognitive techniques such as self-instruction training. Attention, memory, and self-regulation problems were the chief complaints. Four group outcome studies of comprehensive treatment programs are also considered. Overall results gave modest support to the efficacy of cognitive procedures. Findings of the larger scale evaluations were mixed, with two reporting positive and two reporting negative outcomes. 30+ studies.

Selected Positive Trial

Niemann, H., Ruff, R.M., & Baser, C.A. (1990). Computer-assisted attention retraining in head-injured individuals: A controlled efficacy study of an outpatient program. *Journal of Consulting and Clinical Psychology, 58,* **811-817. (rank = 1)**

...biofeedback, relaxation, and cognitive therapy have gained widespread acceptance in the medical world specializing in headache.

Blanchard (p. 548)

HEADACHE

Major Research Reviews in Core Journals

Blanchard, E. (1992). Psychological treatment of benign headache disorders. *Journal of Consulting and Clinical Psychology, 60,* **537-551. (rank = 1)**
The primary nondrug therapies for chronic headache are relaxation training, and EMG and thermal biofeedback. Blanchard concludes that the effectiveness of these methods with both vascular

and tension-type headaches is well established at follow-up periods up to 5 years. Cognitive therapies were superior to other procedures in some studies but less effective in others. Drug and behavioral treatments performed equally in comparative evaluations. The author discusses promising results with thermal biofeedback for pediatric migraine and with audiotape and self-instruction methods for children and adults. 40+ studies.

The initial observation that migraines abated with the administration of propranolol was made fortuitously during a study evaluating this medication for the management of angina.

Holyrod & Penzien (p. 1)

Other Significant Reviews

Holroyd, K., & Penzien, D. (1990). Pharmacological versus nonpharmacological prophylaxis of recurrent migraine headache. A meta-analytic review of clinical trials. *Pain, 42,* 1-13. (rank = 23)
Reviews controlled trials of propranolol, relaxation, biofeedback. Indicates 40-60% improvement for drug, behavioral procedures versus 14% for drug placebo, no improvement for untreated patients. Effect sizes not calculated. Partially supported by grant from National Institutes of Health. 60 studies.

Holroyd, K., & Penzien, D. (1986). Client variables and the behavioral treatment of recurrent tension headache: A meta-analytic review. *Journal of Behavioral Medicine, 9,* 515-536. (rank = 21)
Finds EMG biofeedback, relaxation training, combined treatments superior to control conditions across large number of studies. Significant-

ly greater improvement in patients under 35. Effect sizes not calculated. Partially supported by grant from National Institute of Mental Health. Sessions < 12   37 studies.

Selected Positive Trial

Holroyd, K.A., Nash, J.M., Pingel, J.D., Cordingley, G.E. et al (1991). A comparison of pharmacological (amitriptyline HCL) and nonpharmacological (cognitive-behavioral) therapies for chronic tension headaches. *Journal of Consulting and Clinical Psychology, 59,* 387-393. (rank = 1)

Hostile and socially isolated men appear to benefit most from TAB modification ...

Bennett & Carroll (p. 179)

HEART DISEASE (see also Hypertension, Type A Behavior Pattern)

Major Research Reviews in Core Journals - none

Other Significant Reviews

Bennett, P., & Carroll, D. (1994). Cognitive-behavioural interventions in cardiac rehabilitation. *Journal of Psychosomatic Research, 38,* 169-182. (rank = 16)
Considers outcome studies of cognitive-behavioral treatment, exercise, stress management, smoking cessation, Type A behavior modification. Finds shortterm reduction of post-infarction emotional distress with cognitive pro-

cedures, little consistent evidence of reduced risk for recurrence with any procedures examined. 20+ studies.

Bennett, P., & Carroll, D. (1990). Stress management approaches to the prevention of coronary heart disease. British Journal of Clinical Psychology, 29, 1-12. (rank = 12)

The effects of psychological interventions in patients who have had a myocardial infarction are, at best, modest and there seems little reason to offer such help routinely.

Johnston (p. 453)

Summary of treatment studies concludes stress management effective for mild hypertension, modifying Type A pattern, reducing cholesterol levels in dietary-resistant patients. 30+ studies.

Johnston, D.W. (1985). Psychological interventions in cardiovascular disease. Journal of Psychosomatic Research, 29, 447-456. (rank = 16)

Overview, brief discussion of preventive and postinfarction behavioral, psychoeducational procedures. Relaxation techniques for hypertension, behavior modification for Type A found moderately successful. Biofeedback for hypertension less effective. Partially supported by grants from British Medical Research Council. 20+ studies.

Selected Positive Trial

Frasure-Smith, N., & Prince, R. (1989). Long-term follow-up of the Ischemic Heart Disease Life Stress Monitoring Program. Psychosomatic Medicine, 51, 485-513. (rank = 4)

HOMOSEXUALITY

Major Research Reviews in Core Journals - none

Other Significant Reviews

Haldeman, D. (1994). The practice and ethics of sexual orientation conversion therapy. *Journal of Consulting and Clinical Psychology, 62,* 221- 227. **(rank = 1)**
Reviews studies of psychoanalytic, behavioral treatment for reversing homosexual orientation. Challenges ethical, empirical support. 5+ studies.

Selected Positive Trial

Murphy, T. (1992). Redirecting sexual orientation: Techniques and justifications. *Journal of Sex Research, 29,* 501-523. **(rank = 22)**

Ethicists object to conversion therapy on two grounds: first, that it constitutes a cure for a condition that has been judged not to be an illness, and second, that it reinforces a prejudicial and unjustified devaluation of homosexuality.

Haldeman
(p. 225)

HOSPITALIZATION see Institutionalization

HYPERTENSION (see also Heart Disease, Type A Behavior Pattern)

Major Research Reviews in Core Journals - none

Other Significant Reviews

Kaufmann, P.G., Jacob, R.G., Ewart, C.K., Chesney, M.A. et al (1988). Hypertension intervention pooling project. *Health Psychology, 7 (suppl)*, 209-224. (rank = 8)

Meta-analysis of pooled data shows modest blood pressure declines following biofeedback, relaxation training, other stress reduction techniques. 12 studies.

The evidence for the effectiveness of relaxation and biofeedback therapy has been eroded by the results of recent studies, some of which did not replicate clinically significant treatment effects even on a shortterm basis.

Jacob et al (p. 347)

Jacob, R., Wing, R., & Shapiro, A. (1987). The behavioral treatment of hypertension: Long-term effects. *Behavior Therapy, 18,* 325-352. (rank = 7)

Comprehensive review finds strongest support for weight-loss interventions, modest benefits for sodium restriction, equivocal results for biofeedback, relaxation. Notes few strong studies of exercise, positive effect of clinic monitoring without treatment. Partially supported by grant from National Heart, Lung and Blood Institute. 40+ studies.

Selected Positive Trial

McGrady, A. (1994). Effects of group relaxation training and thermal biofeedback on blood pressure and related physiological and psychological variables in essential hypertension. *Biofeedback and Self-Regulation, 19,* 51-66. (rank = 33)

IMPULSIVITY see Attention-Deficit Hyperactivity Disorder

INSTITUTIONALIZATION

Major Research Reviews in Core Journals

Okun, M., Olding, R., & Cohn, C. (1990). A meta-analysis of subjective well-being interventions among elders. *Psychological Bulletin, 108,* **257-266.** (rank = 3)
Okun et al evaluate a variety of psychosocial techniques involving personal control enhancement, encouragement of social activities, and psychoeducational group work. Most patients were over 70 and living in institutions. Overall, the authors conclude that benefits were modest and shortterm. Effect size = .7 31 studies.

Pfeiffer, S.I., & Strzelecki, S.C. (1990). Inpatient psychiatric treatment of children and adolescents: A review of outcome studies. *Journal of the American Academy of Child and Adolescent Psychiatry, 29,* **847-853.** (rank = 7)
This review uses a quantitative method to identify variables associated with a favorable response to inpatient and residential psychiatric treatment. The bulk of the literature is non-experimental but anecdotal reports are omitted

Psychiatric hospitalization was often beneficial, particularly if a specialized treatment program and aftercare were available.

Pfeiffer & Strzelecki (p. 847)

from the analysis. Lengthy follow-up assessments ranging from 5-15 years were reported in several studies. Analysis of outcome data points to a strong relationship between improvement and the availability of aftercare but only a modest association between outcome and length of stay. 34 studies.

Day-hospital treatment should be evaluated as an important treatment in its own right, because of the potential advantages to the patient, and not simply as a cheap alternative to inpatient care.

Creed et al (p.309)

Creed, F., Black, D., & Anthony, P. (1989). Day-hospital and community treatment for acute psychiatric illness: A critical appraisal. *British Journal of Psychiatry, 154*, 300-310. (rank = 6)
In this review day-hospital and community treatment refer to facilities that provide diagnostic and treatment services as an alternative to inpatient care. They are distinct from day-treatment programs that accommodate special patient groups, and day-centers, whose goal is the maintenance of chronic psychiatric patients. Based on an analysis of outcome data and previous reviews, the authors conclude that day-hospital and community treatment probably had more of an impact on social functioning than on symptom reduction and that potentially lower costs were offset by longer stays for some patients. 10+ studies.

Cournos, F. (1987). Hospitalization outcome studies: Implications for the treatment of the very ill patient. *Psychiatric Clinics of North America, 10*, 165-176. (rank = 30)

Cournos assesses length-of-stay studies, including several that have been particularly influential in guiding the prevailing belief that less is better. Most were conducted with schizophrenic patients, comparing hospitalizations of 10-30 days with extended stays of 2-3 months. Results generally suggested that length of stay had little effect on outcome for cooperative patients who had social supports and who participated in aftercare following discharge. However, the author cautions against overgeneralization of these findings to other populations. 10+ studies.

The movement to close the mental hospitals thus began on a tide of optimism.

O'Driscoll
(p. 8)

Other Significant Reviews

O'Driscoll, C. (1993). The TAPS project: VII. Mental hospital closure: A literature review of outcome studies and evaluative techniques. *British Journal of Psychiatry, 162 (suppl 19),* 7-17. (rank = 6)
Reviews seminal and recent large-scale evaluations of deinstitutionalization effects on chronic mentally ill patients. Identifies "long-stay" group refractory to community care. 20+ studies.

Curry, J.F. (1991). Outcome research on residential treatment: Implications and suggested directions. *American Journal of Orthopsychiatry, 61,* 348-357. (rank = 21)
Surveys inpatient studies of children, adolescents, residential care versus hospitalization

versus community day-treatment. 10+ studies.

Wells, K. (1991). Placement of emotionally disturbed children in residential treatment: A review of placement criteria. *American Journal of Orthopsychiatry, 61,* 339-347. (rank = 21)

Summarizes placement criteria, success predictors from anecdotal reports, earlier literature reviews. 20+ studies.

...use of aftercare services and family and community support after discharge are associated with positive status at follow-up.

Wells (p. 343)

Zimet, S.G., & Farley, G.K. (1985). Day-treatment for children in the United States. *Journal of the American Academy of Child and Adolescent Psychiatry, 24,* 732-738. (rank = 7)

Reviews mostly single-group studies, emotional, behavioral disorders. Reports preliminary positive results. 6 studies.

Selected Positive Trial

Creed, F.H., Anthony, P., Godbert, K., & Huxley, P. (1989). Treatment of severe psychiatric illness in a day-hospital. *British Journal of Psychiatry, 154,* 341-347. (rank = 6)

IRRITABLE BOWEL SYNDROME
see Gastrointestinal Disorders

JUVENILE DELINQUENCY

Major Research Reviews in Core Journals

Yoshikawa, H. (1994). Prevention as cumulative protection: Effects of early family support and education on chronic delinquency and its risks. *Psychological Bulletin, 115,* **28-54. (rank = 3)**
Yoshikawa reviews outcome studies of educational and family programs aimed at preventing chronic delinquency. These programs combined components as varied as problem-solving training and nutritional education, delivered by personnel ranging from paraprofessionals to physicians. Follow-up assessments extended as long as 10 years. The author concludes that several programs obtained modest long-term successes in reducing delinquency. Based on findings of four large and well-designed investigations, Yoshikawa enumerates common elements of successful programs. These included combining school- and home-based interventions, a focus on educational and social competence, provision of parental services such as vocational counseling, inception before age five, and a duration of at least 2 years. 10+ studies.

Parenting variables turned out to be the most powerful predictor of general delinquency.

Yoshikawa (p. 30)

Other Significant Reviews

Although institutional treatment may be necessary for some offenders, community-base d treatment may be appropriate for many more youths.

Mulvey et al (p. 157)

Mulvey, E., Arthur, M., & Reppucci, N. (1993). The prevention and treatment of juvenile delinquency: A review of the research. *Clinical Psychology Review, 13,* 133-167. (rank = 3)
Comprehensive review of findings, policy implications of school, agency, criminal justice programs. Based on background papers prepared for Congressional Office of Technology Assessment. 80+ studies.

Tolan, P., Cromwell, R., & Brasswell, M. (1986). Family therapy with delinquents: A critical review of the literature. *Family Process, 25,* 619-649. (rank = 11)
Concludes behavioral contracting, parent training produced positive effects, generally surpassing psychosocial, criminal justice (e.g. probation) interventions. 20+ studies.

Selected Positive Trial

Henggeler, S.W., Melton, G.B., & Smith, L.A. (1992). Family preservation using multisystemic therapy: An effective alternative to incarcerating serious juvenile offenders. *Journal of Consulting and Clinical Psychology, 60,* 953-961. (rank = 1)

MARITAL AND FAMILY THERAPY

Major Research Reviews in Core Journals

McCallion, P., Toseland, R.W., & Diehl, M. (1994). Social work practice with caregivers of frail older adults. Research on Social Work Practice, 4, 64-88. (rank = 8)
McCallion et al review outcome research on interventions for the elderly and for caregiving family members. Consultation, coordination, case management, and counseling services are included. The authors interpret outcome data on individual and group counseling, and respite and day care programs as supporting a moderate benefit to family members. They find no clear evidence that case management had a consistent impact on health care utilization, mortality, or quality of life in the research reviewed. 20+ studies.

Effect sizes appear to be largest when the treatment first appears and then drop as the studies are replicated...

Jacobson & Addis (p. 86)

Jacobson, N., & Addis, M. (1993). Research on couples and couple therapy: What do we know? Where are we going? Journal of Consulting and Clinical Psychology, 61, 85-93. (rank = 1)
In this status report on marital and couple therapy, Jacobson and Addis briefly highlight research on a number of treatment approaches. They conclude that behavioral couple therapy received consistent empirical support in numerous controlled studies. Promising results were also

obtained with emotion-focused and insight-oriented couple therapy, although relatively few controlled trials were reported. Success appeared to be inversely related to age, and to levels of distress and depression. Supported by grants from the National Institute of Mental Health. 30+ studies.

Several authors have found that, with a follow-up period over 1 year, there may be significant deterioration of therapy outcome.

Shadish et al (p.1000)

Shadish, W., Montgomery, L., Wilson, P., Wilson, M. et al (1993). Effects of family and marital psycho-therapies: A meta-analysis. *Journal of Consulting and Clinical Psychology, 61,* **992-1002. (rank = 1)**
This massive meta-analysis covers the results of a large number of family (N=101) and marital (N=62) therapy investigations. According to the authors, overall results confirmed the superiority of both types of therapy to no-treatment controls. Assuming equally rigorous design, implementation, and outcome measurement, they consider the various treatment orientations (behavioral, systemic, etc.) to be equally effective, with the exception of humanistic therapies, which are seen as consistently less successful than other approaches. A list of references to the reviewed studies is not included but is available in a separate publication cited by the authors. Partially supported by a grant from the National Institute of Mental Health. Effect size = .5
163 studies.

Hahlweg, K., & Markman, H. (1988). Effectiveness of behavioral marital therapy: Empirical status of be-

havioral techniques in preventing and alleviating marital distress. *Journal of Consulting and Clinical Psychology, 56,* 440-447. (rank = 1)

Hahlweg and Markman provide a meta-analysis of reports on behavioral procedures used therapeutically and preventively in Europe and America. The preventive approach generally involved three to six group sessions conducted by a "leader" or "consultant" rather than a therapist. The authors conclude that behavioral marital therapy was significantly more effective than no treatment, yielding improvement rates around 70% which were maintained at 3-12 month follow-up. The preventive interventions also proved superior to control techniques in improving premarital relationships and forestalling subsequent problems. Partially supported by a grant from the National Institute of Mental Health. Effect size for therapy = 1.0   Effect size for prevention = .8   17 therapy studies; 7 prevention studies.

The intervention components included in typical programs are communication skill training, problem-solving skill training, and cognitive restructuring.

Hahlweg & Markman (p. 440)

Hazelrigg, M., Cooper, H., & Borduin, C. (1987). Evaluating the effectiveness of family therapies: An integrative review and analysis. *Psychological Bulletin, 101,* 428-442. (rank = 3)

This is a quantitative review of controlled outcome studies, all of which included comparisons to either an alternative treatment, waiting-list group, or placebo. Like the above reviews, Hazelrigg et al confirm that family interventions produced significantly higher improvement rates than alternative or no-treatment procedures both at the conclusion of therapy and at follow-up periods to 3 years. In addition, multidimensional gains were common, with improvement noted on target problems as well as in other areas of family functioning. A useful summary table of 10 previous reviews of the family therapy literature is provided. Effect size = .5 20 studies.

...most family therapists share the assumption that problematic individual behaviors ...are intimately related to patterns of interaction between family members.

Hazelrigg et al (p. 428)

Other Significant Reviews

Beach, S.R.H., Whisman, M.A., & O'Leary, K.D. (1994). Marital therapy for depression: Theoretical foundation, current status, and future directions. *Behavior Therapy, 25,* 345-371. (rank = 7)
Overview of comorbidity issues, detailed assessment of small number of controlled outcome studies. Concludes behavioral marital therapy effective for depression, marital problems when marital discord preceded onset of depression. Partially supported by grant from National Institute of Mental Health. 4 studies.

Wells, R., & Giannetti, V. (1986). Individual marital therapy: A critical re-appraisal. *Family Process, 25,* 43-51. (rank = 11)
Challenges negative assessment of individual marital therapy (i.e. treatment of one partner) in previous reviews. 30+ studies.

Giblin, P., Sprenkle, D.H., & Sheehan, R. (1985). Enrichment outcome research: A meta-analysis of premarital, marital and family interventions. *Journal of Marital and Family Therapy, 11,* 257-271. (rank = 24)
Considers communication, relationship enhancement interventions for nondistressed marriages, families. Notes modest positive results. List of studies not included, available from authors. Effect size = .4 85 studies.

O'Shea, M.D., & Phelps, R. (1985). Multiple family therapy: Current status and critical appraisal. *Family Process, 24,* 555-582. (rank = 11)
Broad overview of group family therapy plus survey of treatment studies. Some positive findings. 5+ studies.

Selected Positive Trial

Snyder, D.K., & Wills, R.M. (1989). Behavioral versus insight-oriented marital therapy: Effects on individual and interspousal functioning. *Journal of Consulting and Clinical Psychology, 57,* 39-46. (rank = 1)

A review of multiple family therapy indicated that the approach was prospering but was confined to isolated pockets of clinical practice.

O'Shea & Phelps (p. 555)

MEDICAL PROCEDURES

Major Research Reviews in Core Journals

Patients in the distraction condition played a video ping-pong game ...during dental sessions.

Ludwick-Rosenthal & Neufeld (p. 334)

Ludwick-Rosenthal, R., & Neufeld, R. (1988). Stress management during noxious medical procedures: An evaluative review of outcome studies. *Psychological Bulletin, 104,* 326-342. (rank = 3)
This review considers four types of intervention for reducing anxiety and discomfort during medical procedures: provision of information; relaxation training; cognitive techniques including distraction and enhancement of perceived control; and modeling. Medical situations included dental treatment, blood donations, and various gastrointestinal and gynecological diagnostic techniques. Most trials used some form of experimental control and a combination of self-report, behavioral, and physiological outcome measures. The authors find strongest support for cognitive-behavioral and modeling approaches. Supported by grants from the Canadian government. 30+ studies.

Other Significant Reviews

Tarnowski, K., Rasnake, L., & Drabman, R. (1987). Behavioral assessment and treatment of pediatric burn injuries: A review. *Behavior Therapy, 18,* 417-441. (rank = 7)
Analysis of treatment data suggests behavioral techniques promising adjuncts to hydrotherapy, other burn-related procedures. 15+ studies.

Finn, P.E., & Alcorn, J.D. (1986). Noncompliance to hemodialysis dietary regimens: Literature review and treatment recommendations. *Rehabilitation Psychology, 31,* 67-78. (rank = 35)
Reviews mostly single-group, small-scale behavioral studies. Cites generally positive findings. 5+ studies.

Selected Positive Trial

Manne, S.L., Redd, W.H., Jacobsen, P.B., Gorfinkle, K. et al (1990). Behavioral intervention to reduce child and parent distress during venipuncture. *Journal of Consulting and Clinical Psychology, 58,* 565-572. (rank = 1)

Noncompliance to various aspects of dietary regimen can result in... loss in lean body mass or an increase in nitrogenous wastes...

Finn & Alcorn (p. 67)

MEMORY DISORDERS (see also Head Injury)

Major Research Reviews in Core Journals - none

Other Significant Reviews

Godfrey, H.P., & Knight, R.G. (1987). Interventions for amnesiacs: A review. *British Journal of Clinical Psychology, 26,* 83-91. (rank = 29)
Surveys primarily behavioral studies. Finds cognitive-behavioral group methods somewhat effective with brain injured, elderly. 20+ studies.

Selected Positive Trial

Wilson, B.A. (1992). Recovery and compensatory strategies in head-injured memory impaired people several years after insult. *Journal of Neurology, Neurosurgery and Psychiatry, 55,* 177-180. (rank = 7)

Satisfactory outcome is rare with Munchausen's syndrome.

Folks & Freeman (p. 274)

MUNCHAUSEN SYNDROME

Major Research Reviews in Core Journals - none

Other Significant Reviews

Folks, D.G., & Freeman, A.M. (1985). Munchausen's syndrome and other factitious illness. *Psychiatric Clinics of North America, 8,* 263-278. (rank = 30) Overview of diagnostic, treatment issues, summary of numerous case reports. 20+ studies.

Selected Positive Trial

Solyom, C., & Solyom, L. (1990). A treatment program for functional paraplegia/Munchausen syndrome. *Journal of Behavior Therapy and Experimental Psychiatry, 21,* 225-230. (rank = 38)

NIGHTMARES

Major Research Reviews in Core Journals

Halliday, G. (1987). Direct psychological therapies for nightmares: A review. *Clinical Psychology Review, 7,* 501-523. (rank = 3)
Most of the reports considered are behavioral, although a handful of analytic studies are also included. Only two, involving desensitization and relaxation training, used controlled designs. Reductions in nightmare frequency of roughly 80% were obtained in both of these, an improvement rate well above that of control procedures. Sessions < 12   20+ studies.

Selected Positive Trial

Kellner, R., Neidhardt, J., Krakow, B., & Pathak, D. (1992). Changes in chronic nightmares after one session of desensitization or rehearsal instructions. *American Journal of Psychiatry, 149,* 659-663. (rank = 2)

...there is virtually no evidence that clinically significant weight loss can be maintained over the long-term by the vast majority of people.

Garner & Wooley (p. 733)

OBESITY

Major Research Reviews in Core Journals

Garner, D.M., & Wooley, S.C. (1991). Confronting the failure of behavioral and dietary treatments for obesity. *Clinical Psychology Review, 11,* 729-780. (rank = 3)
Garner and Wooley consider outcome data from behavioral weight-loss programs and very low

calorie diets. They also highlight alternative approaches aimed at reducing health risks rather than weight in obese individuals. They note that weight reductions of 10-15 pounds with behavioral methods and up to 40 pounds with very low calorie diets were consistently obtained short-term. However, within 3-5 years virtually all treatment effects were lost in most investigations. Citing these poor long-term outcomes, the authors conclude there is little justification for continued use of either behavioral or dietary treatments of obesity. Partially supported by a grant from the Michigan Health Council. 100+ studies.

Epstein, L.H., & Wing, R.R. (1987). Behavioral treatment of childhood obesity. *Psychological Bulletin, 101,* 331-341. (rank = 3)

The behavioral procedures used most frequently with childhood obesity emphasize diet, exercise, behavior modification to promote appropriate eating habits, and parent training. Epstein and Wing consider trials of these procedures with children and adolescents 1 to 18 years of age. Most used controlled designs in which behavioral methods were compared to no treatment or placebo in a clinical setting. Four were large-scale school-based evaluations. Overall findings were positive, with behavioral interventions typically producing a 10% reduction in percentage overweight, a significantly greater decline than in control conditions. Parental involvement was identified as a predictor of success. Partially supported by grants from the National Institute of Child Health and Human Development. 24 studies.

Smith, M.E., & Fremouw, W.J. (1987). A realistic approach to treating obesity. *Clinical Psychology Review, 7,* **449-465. (rank = 3)**
This paper presents a detailed examination of biobehavioral factors in obesity and a brief review of the weight-loss literature. Although results were generally discouraging, the authors find some grounds for optimism in studies of people who succeeded in weight-loss programs. Analysis of these studies yielded a number of success predictors including high basal metabolic rate, adult-onset obesity, and a history of minimal dietary failure. 10+ studies.

Obese individuals with a poor prognosis may then be more realistically treated by placing an emphasis on the development of a healthy lifestyle and self-concept while de-emphasizing weight loss as the primary goal.

Smith & Fremouw (p. 449)

Other Significant Reviews

Black, D.R., Gleser, L.J., & Kooyers, K.J. (1990) A meta-analytic evaluation of couples weight-loss programs. *Health Psychology, 9,* **330-347. (rank = 8)**
Finds slight advantage for behavioral weight-loss programs when partner participated for emotional, maintenance support. Partially funded by grant from National Science Foundation. 12 studies.

Whisman, M.A. (1990). The efficacy of booster maintenance sessions in behavior therapy: Review and methodological critique. *Clinical Psychology Review, 10,* 155-170. (rank = 3)

... therapist- and spouse-controlled exposure in vivo were not related to larger effect sizes than self-controlled exposure in vivo.

van Blakom et al (p. 374)

Reviews controlled trials of behavioral follow-up procedures designed to prolong improvement. Includes alcoholism, depression, smoking cessation, weight loss. Reports modest effect in 50% of studies. Supported by grant from National Institute of Mental Health. 30 studies.

Selected Positive Trial

Epstein, L.H., McCurley, J., Wing, R.R., & Valoski, A. (1990). Five-year follow-up of family-based behavioral treatments for childhood obesity. *Journal of Consulting and Clinical Psychology, 58,* 661-664. (rank = 1)

OBSESSIVE-COMPULSIVE DISORDER

Major Research Reviews in Core Journals

van Blakom, A.J., van Oppen, P., Vermeulen, A., van Dyck, R. et al (1994). A meta-analysis on the treatment of obsessive-compulsive disorder: A comparison of antidepressants, behavior, and cognitive therapy. *Clinical Psychology Review, 14,* 359-381. (rank = 3)

This paper considers controlled trials of the standard drug and nondrug treatments used individually and in combination. The authors divide their analysis into results based on self-assessed improvement and results based on ratings by independent assessors. On both types of outcome measure, improvement rates were found to be considerably higher for serotonergic antidepressants and behavioral procedures than for placebo. Behavior therapy produced significantly greater gains than drug therapy on self-assessment but not on observer-based measures of improvement. The combination of drug and nondrug procedures also showed a trend toward higher improvement rates than drug therapy alone on self-assessment. Effect size for drugs (independent assessor) = 1.6 Effect size for behavior therapy (independent assessor) = 1.5 Effect size for cognitive therapy (independent assessor) = 1.0 86 studies.

Obsessive-compulsive disorder was once regarded as a condition with an unfavorable prognosis ... however, two treatments are now believed to be effective.

Christensen et al (p. 701)

Christensen, H., Chadzi, P.D., Andrews, G., & Mattick, R. (1987). Behavior therapy and tricyclic medication in the treatment of obsessive-compulsive disorder: A quantitative review. *Journal of Consulting and Clinical Psychology, 55,* **701-711. (rank = 1)**
Christensen et al conduct a meta-analysis of studies which assessed the effectiveness of exposure-based interventions and drug therapy (primarily clomipramine). None directly com-

pared the two modalities. Like the preceding paper, this analysis indicates that both forms of treatment were associated with appreciable reductions in obsessive-compulsive symptoms and that these reductions were significantly greater than improvements with control procedures such as relaxation training. Substantial declines in depression were also observed with both types of therapy. A list of references to reviewed studies is not included but can be obtained from the authors. Sessions < 12 Effect size = 1.0 71 studies.

Optimally, role-playing under the supervision of the therapist can help family members and the patients themselves to understand which interventions are helpful and which might be counterproductive with regard to homework.

Jenike & Rauch (p. 15)

Other Significant Reviews

Jenike, M.A., & Rauch, S.L. (1994). Managing the patient with treatment-resistant obsessive-compulsive disorder: Current strategies. *Journal of Clinical Psychiatry, 55 (3, suppl),* **11-17. (rank = 5)**
Overview of drug, behavioral treatments, briefly highlights outcome research. Concludes minimum treatment length 20 hours for exposure and response prevention, 10 hours for drug therapy. Detailed treatment recommendations included. [See Jenike (1990) below for discussion of earlier research.] 30+ studies.

Abel, J.L. (1993). Exposure with response prevention and serotonergic antidepressants in the treatment of obsessive-compulsive disorder: A review and implications for interdisciplinary treat-

ment. *Behaviour Research and Therapy, 31,* 463-478. (rank = 9)
Reviews drug, behavioral studies, including six direct comparisons. Suggests exposure plus response prevention more effective for rituals, clomipramine useful for severe depression.
20+ studies.

Zetin, M., & Kramer, M.A. (1992). Obsessive-compulsive disorder. *Hospital and Community Psychiatry, 43,* 689-699. (rank = 19)
Comprehensive overview, survey of treatment research. Emphasizes pharmacotherapy, clinical decision-making, augmentation strategies, use of behavior therapy to extend drug benefits.
30+ studies.

Jenike, M.A. (1990). Approaches to the patient with treatment-refractory obsessive-compulsive disorder. *Journal of Clinical Psychiatry, 51, (2 suppl),* 15-21. (rank = 5)
Cites mostly pharmacological studies. Concludes most patients labeled treatment-resistant received inadequate medication, behavior therapy. Flowchart for treatment decisions included. [For update see Jenike and Rauch (1994) above.]
20+ studies.

... the most common symptoms among children are concern about dirt or germs ... and repeating and checking behaviors.

Zetin & Kramer (p. 690)

Insel, T.R. (1985). Obsessive-compulsive disorder. Psychiatric Clinics of North America, 8, 105-117. (rank = 30)
Background paper covers differential diagnosis, epidemiology, biology, genetics, relation to depression. Reviews drug trials, notes benefits, shortcomings of pharmacotherapy, role of behavioral treatments. 5 studies.

Unfortunately, discontinuing the medication, even after a year of treatment, may precipitate a relapse.

Insel
(p. 114)

Selected Positive Trial

Hiss, H., Foa, E.B., & Kozak, M.J. (1994). Relapse prevention program for treatment of obsessive-compulsive disorder. Journal of Consulting and Clinical Psychology, 62, 801-808. (rank = 1)

PAIN MANAGEMENT

Major Research Reviews in Core Journals

Keefe, F.J., Dunsmore, J., & Burnett, R. (1992). Behavioral and cognitive-behavioral approaches to chronic pain: Recent advances and future directions. Journal of Consulting and Clinical Psychology, 60, 528-536. (rank = 1)
Keefe et al review outcome evaluations of seven hospital-based multidisciplinary pain programs in this extensive overview paper. Fordyce's pioneering work at the University of Washington

and a large-scale evaluation at the Mayo Clinic
are included. Most of the programs involved outpatients suffering from chronic back pain. The
authors interpret results as encouraging, with
significant declines in narcotic use, downtime,
and unemployment reported in most investigations. They note a paucity of placebo and
other controls in this research, although the use
of patients with long histories of pain and nonresponse to previous treatments lent credence to
results. 7 studies.

*An important but
neglected topic is
the method used
by physicians to
prepare patients
for behavioral
assessment and
treatment efforts.*

*Keefe et al
(p. 103)*

**Keefe, F.J., Gill, K.M., & Rose, S.C. (1986). Behavior-
al approaches in the multidisciplinary management
of chronic pain: Programs and issues. *Clinical Psychology Review, 6,* 87-113. (rank = 3)**
Behavioral approaches to chronic pain use techniques such as behavioral contracting and spouse
education to modify social factors that exacerbate
pain. Cognitive-behavioral strategies emphasize
attitude change and the development of coping
skills. This paper reviews controlled studies of
the two approaches in comparison with each other and with nonpsychological methods such as
physical therapy. Prevention and the role of
drugs in combination treatments are also covered. According to the authors, findings of clinical trials supported the superiority of behavioral
and cognitive-behavioral treatments to control
conditions, with no clear advantage to either.
Prevention studies yielded some promising re-

sults, while those that combined drugs and psychological methods were inconclusive. Supported by grants from the National Institute of Mental Health and the National Institute of Arthritis, Diabetes, and Digestive and Kidney Diseases. 20+ studies.

Other Significant Reviews

Flor, H., Fydrich, T., & Turk, D.C. (1992). Efficacy of multidisciplinary pain treatment centers: A meta-analytic review. *Pain, 49,* 221-230. (rank = 23)
Evaluates outcome studies of multidisciplinary treatment programs, mostly inpatient, chronic back pain. Finds 50% improvement at 2-year follow-up with combined medical, psychological, behavioral procedures. Superior to no treatment, waiting-list, medical, physical therapy alone. Supported by grant from German government. Effect size = .6 65 studies.

Benjamin, S. (1989). Psychological treatment of chronic pain: A selective review. *Journal of Psychosomatic Research, 33,* 121-131. (rank = 16)
Highlights psychiatric, legal, family issues, controlled studies. Multidisciplinary treatment considered especially beneficial. 5+ studies.

The beneficial effects of multidisciplinary treatment were not limited to improvements in pain, mood and interference but also extended to behavioral variables such as return to work or use of the health care system.

Flor et al (p. 221)

Malone, M.D., & Strube, M.J. (1988). Meta-analysis of nonmedical treatments for chronic pain. *Pain, 34,* 231-244. (rank = 23)
Techniques included autogenic and relaxation training, cognitive therapy, hypnosis, operant conditioning, biofeedback. Finds biofeedback, combination methods modestly effective. Effect size for combination methods = 1.3 48 studies in meta-analysis; 61 other reports summarized.

Selected Positive Trial

Flor, H., & Birbaumer, N. (1993). Comparison of the efficacy of electromyographic biofeedback, cognitive-behavioral therapy, and conservative medical interventions in the treatment of chronic musculoskeletal pain. *Journal of Consulting and Clinical Psychology, 61,* 653-658. (rank = 1)

Onset is normally in the late twenties to early thirties, and is generally precipitated by situational stressors.

Acierno et al (p. 567)

PANIC DISORDER – Behavior Therapy

Major Research Reviews in Core Journals

Acierno, R.E., Hersen, M., & van Hasselt, V.B. (1993). Interventions for panic disorder: A critical review of the literature. *Clinical Psychology Review, 13,* 561-578. (rank = 3)
Acierno et al provide a detailed evaluation of well-designed studies of cognitive, behavioral, and multicomponent interventions. All trials re-

ported highly positive results, with as many as 80% of patients found to be panic-free at follow-up periods of up to 2 years. The combination of cognitive therapy, exposure-based relaxation, and breathing retraining procedures was generally found to be more effective than individual application of any of these techniques. 5+ studies.

... it appears that respiratory control techniques have specific effects on the alleviation of panic attacks.

Rapee (p. 432)

Rapee, R. (1987). The psychological treatment of panic attacks: Theoretical conceptualization and review of evidence. *Clinical Psychology Review, 7,* 427-438. (rank = 3)

Rapee sets out a detailed rationale for the behavioral treatment of panic disorder and reviews a number of clinical trials. Three procedures are highlighted: breathing retraining, alteration of catastrophic misinterpretations of symptoms, and exposure to somatic sensations. The author finds strongest empirical support for the use of breathing techniques, including one controlled investigation in which breathing retraining plus exposure proved superior to exposure alone. Several reports in which administration of carbon dioxide was used for symptom production and habituation are also discussed. 5+ studies.

Other Significant Reviews

Trull, T.J., Nietzel, M.T., & Main, A. (1988). The use of meta-analysis to assess the clinical significance of behavior therapy for agoraphobia. *Behavior Therapy, 19,* **527-538. (rank = 7)**
Uses meta-analytic technique focused on clinical rather than statistical significance of results. Finds behavioral methods moderately effective, group, individual treatment roughly equal. List of studies not included. 19 studies.

Percentage of agoraphobic subjects in the sample and duration of the illness were unrelated to effect size.

Clum et al (p. 317)

Selected Positive Trial

Barlow, D.H., Craske, M.G., Cerny, J.A., & Klosko, J.S. (1989). Behavioral treatment of panic disorder. *Behavior Therapy, 20,* **261-282. (rank = 7)**

PANIC DISORDER – Behavior Therapy   and Drug Therapy

Major Research Reviews in Core Journals

Clum, G.A., Clum G.A., & Surls, R. (1993). Meta-analysis of treatments for panic disorder. *Journal of Consulting and Clinical Psychology, 61,* **317-326. (rank = 1)**

This meta-analysis focuses on controlled outcome studies of drug, psychological, and combined interventions. Trials were about equally divided between psychological and pharmacological treatments. The authors conclude that cognitive-, exposure-, and relaxation-based methods produced the most consistent gains. Flooding and the combination of drug and psychological procedures were particularly effective. Among drug interventions, antidepressants were found to be more successful than high-potency benzodiazepines. Effect size for coping techniques = 1.4 Effect size for flooding = 1.4 Effect size for antidepressants = .8 Effect size for combination treatments = 1.1 29 studies.

In vivo exposure is a useful and perhaps necessary treatment for panic disorder with agoraphobia...

Michelson & Marchione (p. 101)

Michelson, L.K., & Marchione, K. (1991). Behavioral, cognitive, and pharmacological treatments of panic disorder with agoraphobia: Critique and synthesis. *Journal of Consulting and Clinical Psychology, 59,* 100-114. (rank = 1)

Michelson and Marchione review behavioral trials which included programmed practice instruction, imagery, in vivo exposure, flooding, and relaxation training. Drug studies of tricyclics, monoamine oxidase inhibitors, beta-blockers, and low- and high-potency benzodiazepines are also covered. Exposure-based methods were most widely tested and found to be moderately to highly effective whether administered individually or in groups. Of the drugs tested, antidepressants proved superior to placebo and more effective than beta-blockers and benzodiazepines in several studies. The combination of pharmacotherapy and behavioral treatment led to greater improvement than either modality alone in some studies, although high attrition and relapse rates were associated with the medication component. Based on an "overall efficacy index," cognitive therapy plus graduated exposure ranked most effective while benzodiazepines were least effective of the various treatments assessed. Supported in part by a grant from the National Institute of Mental Health. 30+ studies.

Antidepressants can be valuable in patients who fail with exposure treatment, refuse it, or are dysphoric...

Marks & O'Sullivan (p. 656)

Marks, I., & O'Sullivan, G. (1988). Drugs and psychological treatments for agoraphobia/panic and obsessive-compulsive disorders: A review. *British Journal of Psychiatry, 153,* **650-658. (rank = 6)**
In contrast to the comprehensive analyses above, Marks and O'Sullivan present a succinct review of drug trials along with a detailed discussion of the advantages and disadvantages of drug and exposure-based therapies. They conclude that the cost-effectiveness, lack of side effects, and long-term gains demonstrated by exposure-based therapy make this the first line treatment for the three disorders considered. Sessions < 12 20+ studies.

Other Significant Reviews

Cox, B.J., Endler, N.S., Lee, P.S., & Swinson, R.P. (1992). A meta-analysis of treatments for panic dis-

order with agoraphobia: Imipramine, alprazolam, and in vivo exposure. *Journal of Behavior Therapy and Experimental Psychiatry, 23,* 175-182. (rank = 38)

Reviews controlled studies, concludes exposure, alprazolam effective. Alprazolam less useful for agoraphobic symptoms, imipramine generally ineffective. [See following paper for positive assessment of imipramine.] Effect size for exposure = 3.4 Effect size for alprazolam = 2.1 34 studies.

It was also clear that only limited improvement can be expected from behavior therapies that do not involve exposure to the symptoms of panic or to the feared situation.

Mattick et al (p. 567)

Mattick, R.P., Andrews, G., Hadzi-Pavlovic, D., & Christensen, H. (1990). Treatment of panic and agoraphobia: An integrative review. *Journal of Nervous and Mental Disease, 178,* 567-576. (rank = 11)

Meta-analysis concludes substantial improvement in panic symptoms with imipramine, alprazolam, in vivo exposure, especially combined with cognitive therapy. Limited support for low-potency benzodiazepines, monoamine oxidase inhibitors. Partially supported by grant from Australian government. [See preceding paper for negative assessment of imipramine.] Effect size for drug therapy, exposure = 1.0 51 studies.

Clum, G.A. (1989). Psychological interventions versus drugs in the treatment of panic. *Behavior Therapy, 20,* 429-457. (rank = 7)

Evaluates studies of behavioral, drug, combined therapies. Finds highest success, lowest relapse rates with behavioral procedures. High-potency benzodiazapines effective but greater risk of relapse. 50+ studies.

Lydiard, R.B., & Ballenger, J.C. (1987). Antidepressants in panic disorder and agoraphobia. Journal of Affective Disorders, 13, 153-168. (rank = 16)
Covers treatment research on pharmacotherapy alone, in combination with behavior therapy. Like Mattick et al (1990) above, concludes combination treatment generally superior. Negative drug studies discussed. 12+ studies.

Selected Positive Trial

Hegel, M.T., Ravaris, C.L., & Ahles, T.A. (1994). Combined cognitive-behavioral and time-limited alprazolam treatment of panic disorder. Behavior Therapy, 25, 183-185. (rank = 7)

There is strong evidence that panic disorder occurs in children and adolescents and that its clinical presentation in this population is similar to that found in adults.

Moreau & Weissman
(p. 1306)

PANIC DISORDER – Pediatric

Major Research Reviews in Core Journals

Moreau, D., & Weissman, M.M. (1992). Panic disorder in children and adolescents: A review. American Journal of Psychiatry, 149, 1306-1314. (rank = 2)
Moreau and Weissman provide a comprehensive description of panic disorder in children and adolescents, with an emphasis on epidemiology, bio-

logical underpinnings, and treatment. They identify a sparse treatment literature consisting exclusively of drug trials. Several of these obtained positive results with antianxiety and antidepressant medication. The authors could locate no reports on the use of nonpharmacological methods with this population. Partially supported by grants from the National Institute of Mental Health. 6 studies.

The power of paradoxical interventions for breaking vicious circles and for helping more severe cases has often been claimed but has rarely been directly tested.

Shoham-Solomon & Rosenthal (p. 26)

Selected Positive Trial

Ballenger, J.C., Carey, D.J., Steele, J.J., & Cornish-McTighe, D. (1989). Three cases of panic disorder with agoraphobia in children. *American Journal of Psychiatry, 146,* 922-925. (rank = 2)

PARADOXICAL INTERVENTIONS

Major Research Reviews in Core Journals

Shoham-Solomon, V., & Rosenthal, R. (1987). Paradoxical interventions: A meta-analysis. *Journal of Consulting and Clinical Psychology, 55,* 22-28. (rank = 1)
Paradoxical interventions are procedures that encourage, praise, or prescribe the very behaviors or symptoms the patient wishes to alter. They are used as adjuncts in behavioral and family therapy. Results of this meta-analysis suggest that in most trials paradoxical interventions

were significantly more effective than no treatment or various control manipulations when added to cognitive and behavioral procedures. Treatments for agoraphobia, insomnia, and depression are highlighted. Effect size = .4   10 studies.

Selected Positive Trial

Mersch, P.P., Hildebrand, M., Lavy, E.H., Wessel, I. et al (1992). Somatic symptoms in social phobia: A treatment method based on rational emotive therapy and paradoxical interventions. *Journal of Behavior Therapy and Experimental Psychiatry, 23,* **199-211. (rank = 38)**

Do PET parents in fact learn the specific communication skills taught, and does this have any measurable effect on their behavior and attitudes...?

Cedar & Levant
(p. 373)

PARENT EFFECTIVENESS TRAINING

Major Research Reviews in Core Journals -None

Other Significant Reviews

Cedar, B., & Levant, R.F. (1990). A meta-analysis of the effects of parent effectiveness training. *The American Journal of Family Therapy, 18,* **373-384. (rank = 47)**
Examines mostly unpublished studies, dissertations. Finds PET marginally more effective than control conditions. List of reviewed studies not included, available from authors. Effect size = .3 26 studies.

Berry, M. (1988). A review of parent training programs in child welfare. *Social Service Review, 62,* 302-23. (rank = 5)

Evaluates programs for foster parents, adoptive parents, reunified families. Notes moderate success with behavioral procedures, lower rates for psychoeducational methods. 20+ studies.

Selected Positive Trial

Long, P., Forehand, R., Wierson, M, & Morgan, A. (1994). Does parent training with young noncompliant children have long-term effects? *Behaviour Research and Therapy 32,* 101-107. (rank = 9)

Factors contributing importantly to suicide in borderline personality disorder patients include continuing alcohol abuse ... and a history of parental brutality or sexual molestation.

Stone (p. 303)

PERSONALITY DISORDERS

Major Research Reviews in Core Journals

Stone, M.H. (1993). Long-term outcome in personality disorders. *British Journal of Psychiatry, 162,* 299-313. (rank = 6)

Stone provides an overview of long-term follow-up studies, some exceeding 20 years. Most dealt with inpatients suffering from borderline, antisocial, or schizotypal disorders. The author finds outcomes with borderline patients most positive and results with schizoid, schizotypal, and antisocial disorders least promising. 61 studies.

Other Significant Reviews

Piper, A. (1994). Multiple personality disorder. British Journal of Psychiatry 164, 600-612. (rank = 6)
Comprehensive overview covers diagnosis, skepticism regarding alleged increasing prevalence, relation to sexual abuse, malpractice issues. Small treatment literature. 5+ studies.

The aim of psychotherapy may as often be the reduction of suicide risk as the alleviation of symptoms...

Higgitt & Fonagy (p. 38)

Paris, J. (1993). The treatment of borderline personality disorder in light of the research on its long-term outcome. Canadian Journal of Psychiatry, 38, (suppl 1), 28-34. (rank = 28)
Broad review of treatment research, long-term studies of natural history. Notes majority of patients significantly improved by middle age, 10% suicide rate. 5+ studies.

Higgitt, A., & Fonagy, P. (1992). Psychotherapy in borderline and narcissistic personality disorder. British Journal of Psychiatry, 161, 23-43. (rank = 6)
Considers studies of psychoanalysis, supportive psychotherapy, group and family therapy, cognitive-behavioral methods, inpatient and combination treatments. Finds group techniques generally inappropriate. 20+ studies.

Reich, J.H., & Green, A.I. (1991). Effect of personality disorders on outcome of treatment. Journal of Nervous and Mental Disease, 179, 74-82. (rank = 11)

Reviews treatment studies of patients with Axis I and personality disorder. Notes poorer response to treatment for depression, panic disorder, other conditions when personality disorder present. 22 studies.

A recent study found ...that PTSD may be more common than such disorders as drug abuse and depression.

Solomon et al (p. 633)

Aronson, T.A. (1989). A critical review of psychotherapeutic treatments of the borderline personality: Historical trends and future directions. *Journal of Nervous and Mental Disease, 177,* **511-528. (rank = 11)**

Details psychoanalytic, group, family, behavioral approaches. Cites empirical studies, treatment risks for certain patients. 5+ studies.

Selected Positive Trial

Winston, A., Laikin, M., Pollack, J., Samstag, L.W. et al (1994). Short-term psychotherapy of personality disorders. *American Journal of Psychiatry, 151,* **190-194. (rank = 2)**

POSTTRAUMATIC STRESS DISORDER

Major Research Reviews in Core Journals

Solomon, S.D., Gerrity, E.T., & Muff, A.M. (1992). Efficacy of treatments for posttraumatic stress disorder: An empirical review. *JAMA: Journal of the*

**American Medical Association, 268, 633-638.
(rank = 4)**
This review considers outcome studies of drug treatment, psychotherapy, and behavioral methods. All used controlled designs in which an active procedure was compared to alternative forms of therapy or a no-treatment condition. The majority of patients were combat veterans, with rape victims and the profoundly bereaved also represented. Based on their analysis of outcomes, the authors conclude there were significant gains with behavioral methods, particularly exposure-based techniques. They describe the effects of drug therapy as weaker, but clinically meaningful. Cognitive, psychodynamic, and hypnotic procedures also appeared to offer some promise. 6 nondrug studies; 5 drug studies.

A gradual exposure to group psychotherapy should be considered. Too rapid movement into group psychotherapy may overwhelm impaired resources, producing secondary traumatization.

*Allen & Bloom
(p. 427)*

Other Significant Reviews

**Allen, S.N., & Bloom, S.L. (1994). Group and family treatment of posttraumatic stress disorder. *Psychiatric Clinics of North America, 17,* 425-437.
(rank = 30)**
Comprehensive overview of theoretical issues, educational, psychodynamic, family approaches. Brief discussion of sparse outcome literature. 5 studies.

McFarlane, A.C. (1994). Individual psychotherapy for posttraumatic stress disorder. *Psychiatric Clinics of*

North America, 17, 393-408. (rank = 30)
Like preceding paper, provides comprehensive overview. Describes natural history, comorbidity, selected outcome reports. 10 studies.

The overall picture emerging from the literature on the aftermath of rape indicates that virtually all of the symptoms which define posttraumatic stress disorder appear in rape victims.

Steketee & Foa (p. 73)

Steketee, G., & Foa, B.D. (1987). Rape victims: Posttraumatic stress responses and their treatment: A review of the literature. *Journal of Anxiety Disorders, 1,* 69-86. (rank = 17)
Covers research on emotional consequences, predictors of adjustment, treatment effectiveness. Includes desensitization, flooding, cognitive-behavioral, psychodynamic therapy. Most studies anecdotal, uncontrolled, moderate improvement reported. 10+ studies.

Ettedgui, E., & Bridges, M. (1985). Posttraumatic stress disorder. *Psychiatric Clinics of North America, 8,* 89-103. (rank = 30)
Overview of historical issues, relation to other psychiatric disorders, differential diagnosis. Brief summary of numerous treatment reports. 20+ studies.

Selected Positive Trial

Marmar, C.R. (1991). Brief dynamic psychotherapy of posttraumatic stress disorder. *Psychiatric Annals, 21,* 405-414. (rank = 42)

PREMENSTRUAL SYNDROME

Major Research Reviews in Core Journals

Blumenthal, S.J., & Nadelson, C.C. (1988). Late luteal phase dysphoric disorder (premenstrual syndromes): Clinical implications. *Journal of Clinical Psychiatry, 49,* 469-474. (rank = 5)

Blumenthal and Nadelson cover the historical context of premenstrual syndrome, diagnostic criteria, etiology, and treatment research. The outcome studies cited are all pharmacologic. Findings were generally negative for progesterone therapy and inconclusive for vitamin, diuretic, and oral contraceptive approaches. Psychotropic drugs such as alprazolam showed some promise. 10+ studies.

The term premenstrual syndromes is used because researchers believe that there may be several subtypes of the disorder characterized by different clusters of symptoms.

Blumenthal & Nadelson (p. 469)

Other Significant Reviews

Rausch, J.L., & Parry, B.L. (1993). Treatment of premenstrual mood symptoms. *Psychiatric Clinics of North America, 16,* 829-839. (rank = 30)

Briefly surveys nutritional, hormonal therapies, use of antianxiety, antidepressant drugs. Indicates 50% improvement rate with conservative measures such as exercise, caffeine avoidance, stress management. 40 studies.

Robinson, G.E., & Garfinkel, P.E. (1990). Problems in the treatment of premenstrual syndrome. *Canadian*

Journal of Psychiatry, 35, 199-206. (rank = 28)
Like preceding reviews, finds little support for vitamin, diuretic, hormonal therapy, possible role for benzodiazepines. Outlines conservative management with brief counseling, exercise, diet, stress reduction. 10+ studies.

...most studies used highly experienced therapists. In four studies, the average length of postgraduate clinical experience was more than 9 years.

Crits-Christoph (p. 153)

Selected Positive Trial

Steege, J.F., & Blumenthal, J.A. (1993). The effects of aerobic exercise on premenstrual symptoms in middle-aged women: A preliminary study. *Journal of Psychosomatic Research 37,* 127-133. (rank = 16)

PSYCHODYNAMIC THERAPY

Major Research Reviews in Core Journals

Crits-Christoph, P. (1992). The efficacy of brief dynamic psychotherapy: A meta-analysis. *American Journal of Psychiatry, 149,* 151-158. (rank = 2)
Crits-Christoph considers controlled studies (publications and conference presentations) which compared brief, manual-based, psychodynamic therapy to either an alternative form of psychotherapy, drug therapy, or no treatment. Treated conditions included depression, substance abuse, and personality disorders. Overall, the author judges brief dynamic therapy to be considerably more effective than no treatment and approximately equal in results to the other

therapies tested. Partially supported by grants from the National Institute of Mental Health. Effect size = 1.1   11 studies.

Svartberg, M., & Stiles, T.C. (1991). Comparative effects of shortterm psychodynamic psychotherapy: A meta-analysis. *Journal of Consulting and Clinical Psychology, 59,* 704-714. (rank = 1)
Although this review addresses essentially the same treatment as Crits-Christoph (1992) above, Svartberg and Stiles examine a larger and more heterogeneous set of studies. Presenting complaints included medical problems, eating disorders, depression, anxiety, and substance abuse. In contrast to the preceding paper, the trials considered in this review did not necessarily involve use of a treatment manual. Unlike Crits-Christoph the present authors find that psychodynamic methods produced only slight gains, exceeding those of no-treatment controls, but inferior to the effects of alternative therapies both at posttreatment and 1-year follow-up. Partially supported by a grant from the Norwegian government. [For additional discussion of these two reviews see below.] 19 studies.

... more than 20 shortterm psychodynamic psychotherapy variants exist that conceptually originate from psychodynamic or psychoanalytic theory.

Svartberg & Stiles
(p. 704)

Crits-Christoph, P. (1993). "Efficacy of brief dynamic psychotherapy": Reply. *American Journal of Psychiatry, 150,* 173-174, 684-685. (rank = 2)

Svartberg, M., & Stiles, T.C. (1993). "Efficacy of brief dynamic psychotherapy": Comments. *American Journal of Psychiatry, 150,* 684-685. (rank = 2)

Testani, M. (1993). "Efficacy of brief dynamic psychotherapy": Comments. *American Journal of Psychiatry, 150,* 173-174. (rank = 2)

Selected Positive Trial

Smyrnios, K.X., & Kirkby, R.J. (1993). Long-term comparison of brief versus unlimited psychodynamic treatments with children and their parents. *Journal of Consulting and Clinical Psychology, 61,* 1020-1027. (rank = 1)

Rational emotive therapy ...is characterized by the use of problem-oriented techniques only after the client has been confronted with his or her irrational ideas...

Engels et al (p. 1083)

RATIONAL EMOTIVE THERAPY

Major Research Reviews in Core Journals

Engels, G.I., Garnefski, N., & Diekstra, R.F.W. (1993). Efficacy of rational emotive therapy: A quantitative analysis. *Journal of Consulting and Clinical Psychology, 61,* 1083-1090. (rank = 1)
This meta-analysis deals primarily with anxiety disorders. The authors conclude that, overall, rational emotive therapy significantly outperformed no treatment, with gains roughly equal to those of alternative psychological interventions.

No meaningful differences were found between behaviorally oriented and more exclusively cognitive rational emotive approaches. Effect size = 1.6   28 studies.

Lyons, L.C., & Woods, P.J. (1991). The efficacy of rational emotive therapy: A quantitative review of the outcome research. *Clinical Psychology Review, 11,* 357-369. (rank = 3)

Lyons and Woods focus on a broader range of research than the preceding paper, covering the full spectrum of emotional and behavioral disorders. Results indicate that rational emotive therapy produced significantly greater improvement than control conditions and on an order roughly equal to that of cognitive-behavioral and traditional behavior therapy. The authors observe a significant relationship between treatment duration and degree of improvement. A list of reviewed studies is not included but can be obtained from the authors. Sessions < 12   70 studies.

Effect size was significantly related to therapist experience and to duration of the therapy...

Lyons & Woods (p. 357)

Selected Positive Trial

Emmelkamp, P.M., & Beens, H. (1991). Cognitive therapy with obsessive-compulsive disorder: A comparative evaluation. *Behaviour Research and Therapy, 29,* 293-300. (rank = 9)

RELAXATION TRAINING

Major Research Reviews in Core Journals

With individual relaxation training likely to cost at least twice as much as group training, the gains in treatment efficacy may not justify the higher costs.

Carlson & Hoyle (p. 1065)

Carlson, C.R., & Hoyle, R.H. (1993). Efficacy of abbreviated progressive muscle relaxation training: A quantitative review of behavioral medicine research. *Journal of Consulting and Clinical Psychology, 61,* **1059-1067. (rank = 1)**
This review evaluates research primarily concerned with the use of relaxation procedures in the treatment of headache, hypertension, and reactions to cancer chemotherapy. In general the authors find abbreviated relaxation procedures moderately effective in producing symptomatic relief. Results supported the use of audiotapes to supplement therapist contacts, individual over group administration, and an optimal treatment duration of approximately 12 sessions. Effect size = .9   29 studies.

Other Significant Reviews

Eppley, K.R., & Abrams, A.L. (1989). Differential effects of relaxation techniques on trait anxiety: A meta-analysis. *Journal of Clinical Psychology, 45,* **957-974. (rank = 7)**
Reviews mostly nonclinical reports. Largest effect found with transcendental meditation. List of studies not included, available from authors. Effect size for meditation = .7   Effect size for progressive relaxation = .4   100+ studies.

Selected Positive Trial

Borkovec, T.D., & Costello, E. (1993). Efficacy of applied relaxation and cognitive-behavioral therapy in the treatment of generalized anxiety disorder. *Journal of Consulting and Clinical Psychology, 61,* 611-619. (rank = 1)

...social skills training may be an important factor in earlier release from the hospital.

RESIDENTIAL TREATMENT
see Institutionalization

Benton & Schroeder (p. 744)

SCHIZOPHRENIA

Major Research Reviews in Core Journals

Benton, M.K., & Schroeder, H.E. (1990). Social skills training with schizophrenics: A meta-analytic evaluation. *Journal of Consulting and Clinical Psychology, 58,* 741-747. (rank = 1)

Benton and Schroeder consider outcome reports on behavioral techniques for promoting social skills in schizophrenics. These techniques included modeling, verbal and video feedback, and role-play rehearsal. Most procedures were brief, usually less than 10 hours, and carried out with inpatients. According to the authors, results pointed to significant treatment effects on self-reported assertiveness and social anxiety, as well as on other-rated social behavior. These gains appeared to generalize to naturalistic settings and were associated, in several studies, with improved discharge rates. Effects on general functioning and symptomatology were marginal. Effect size = .8   27 studies.

Mueser, K.T., & Berenbaum, H. (1990). Psychodynamic treatment of schizophrenia: Is there a future? *Psychological Medicine, 20,* 253-262. (rank = 5)

This paper examines a small body of controlled and naturalistic research. Some 350 inpatients participated in these investigations, most treated for 1-2 years. Two of the studies monitored patient progress over a 10-20 year follow-up period. The reviewers consider overall results discouraging, with little improvement noted in most patients in all but one study. A discussion of the possible deleterious effects of treatment for some patients is included. Supported by a grant from the National Institute of Mental Health. 6 studies.

Other Significant Reviews

Alford, B.A., & Correia, C.J. (1994). Cognitive therapy of schizophrenia: Theory and empirical status. *Behavior Therapy, 25,* 17-33. (rank = 7)

Overview includes review of case studies, notes some success in reducing strength of delusional beliefs. 5+ studies.

DeJesus Mari, J., & Streiner, D.L. (1994). An overview of family interventions and relapse on schizophrenia: Meta-analysis of research findings. *Psychological Medicine, 24,* **565-78. (rank = 5)**
Considers controlled trials of brief adjunctive family therapy using psychoeducational procedures. Finds moderate success in reducing relapse, rehospitalization, drug compliance problems. 6 studies.

The psychosocial treatments of choice for schizophrenia... include token economy, social skills training, case management, vocational rehabilitation, and behavioral family therapy.

Liberman et al (p. 91)

Liberman, R.P., Kopelowicz, A., & Young, A.S. (1994). Biobehavioral treatment and rehabilitation of schizophrenia. *Behavior Therapy, 25,* **89-107. (rank = 7)**
Broad overview of combined medical, behavioral interventions. Cites social skills, family management, other clinical trials. 10+ studies.

Birchwood, M. (1992). Early intervention in schizophrenia: Theoretical background and clinical strategies. *British Journal of Clinical Psychology, 31,* **257-278. (rank = 29)**
Emphasizes brief interventions to reduce relapse severity. Describes trials of drug, behavioral, combined methods. 5+ studies.

Breslin, N.A. (1992). Treatment of schizophrenia: Current practice and future promise. *Hospital and Community Psychiatry, 43,* **877-885. (rank = 19)**
Highlights drug studies, including cost considerations. Cites support for adjunctive psychodynamic, family therapy. 40+ studies.

McClellan, J.M., & Werry, J.S. (1992). Schizophrenia. *Psychiatric Clinics of North America, 15,* 131-148. (rank = 30)
Overview of schizophrenia in children, adolescents. Emphasizes drug treatment, including common errors, role of family therapy. 5+ studies.

Many important predictors of outcome have been identified by the North American follow-up studies.

McGlashan (p. 534)

Wasylenki, D.A. (1992). Psychotherapy of schizophrenia revisited. *Hospital and Community Psychiatry, 43,* 123-127 (rank = 19)
Summarizes major outcome studies, adavnces in nondrug treatment. Sees basis for renewed optimism in psychotherapy. 5+ studies.

McGlashan, T.H. (1988). A selective review of recent North American long-term follow-up studies of schizophrenia. *Schizophrenia Bulletin, 14,* 515-542. (rank = 3)
Detailed analysis of studies exceeding 10 years. Suggests plateau reached 5-10 years post-onset, little evidence of consistent treatment effect on natural history of disease. 10 studies.

Strachen, A.M. (1986). Family intervention for the rehabilitation of schizophrenia: Toward protection and coping. *Schizophrenia Bulletin, 12,* 678-698. (rank = 3)
Analyzes controlled family studies combining drug, psychoeducational, behavioral procedures. Significant reductions in relapse rates obtained. 4 studies.

Selected Positive Trial

Bentall, R.P., Haddock, G., & Slade, P.D. (1994). Cognitive behavior therapy for persistent auditory hallucinations: From theory to therapy. *Behavior Therapy, 25.* (rank = 7)

SEASONAL AFFECTIVE DISORDER
see Depression

...subjects receiving self-help interventions are not at greater risk for dropping out of treatment.

Gould & Clum (p. 179)

SELF-HELP

Major Research Reviews in Core Journals

Gould, R.A., & Clum, G.A. (1993). A meta-analysis of self-help treatment approaches. *Clinical Psychology Review, 13,* 169-186. (rank = 3)
Gould and Clum evaluate controlled studies which tested self-help procedures involving books, manuals, or cassettes against no-treatment or placebo controls. Their meta-analysis yields a strong effect for fear reduction and social skills training programs. Positive, but considerably weaker effects, were associated with habit problems such as smoking, drinking, and weight control. The authors note that addition of formal individual therapy generally enhanced the effectiveness of self-help techniques. Effect size = .5   40 studies.

Other Significant Reviews

Scogin, F., Bynum, J., Stephens, G., & Calhoon, S. (1990). Efficacy of self-administered treatment programs: Meta-analytic review. *Professional Psychology: Research and Practice, 21,* 42-47. (rank = 27)
Self- and therapist-administered treatments found equally effective for some disorders. Authors caution against overgeneralization of findings. Effect size = 1.0 40 studies.

... self-injurious behaviour may initially occur for one of a variety of reasons. However, it continues through being reinforced or rewarded...

*Blair
(p. 8)*

Selected Positive Trial

Morawetz, D. (1989). Behavioral self-help treatment for insomnia: A controlled evaluation. *Behavior Therapy, 20,* 365-379. (rank = 7)

SELF-INJURY

Major Research Reviews in Core Journals - none

Other Significant Reviews

Blair, A. (1992). Working with people with learning difficulties who self-injure: A review of the literature. *Behavioural Psychotherapy, 20,* 1-23. (rank = 41)
Broad review of mostly uncontrolled studies of aversive, nonaversive procedures, pharmacotherapy, combined approaches. Concludes no sin-

gle treatment consistently superior, minimally or nonaversive methods preferred. 30+ studies

Winchel, R.M., & Stanley, M. (1991). Self-injurious behavior: A review of the behavior and biology of self-mutilation. *American Journal of Psychiatry,* *148,* **306-317. (rank = 2)**
Emphasizes drug treatment (dopamine, opiate antagonists, tricyclics). Also describes behavioral studies with mentally retarded populations, milieu treatment for borderline, other character disorders. Partially supported by grant from National Institute of Mental Health. 30+ studies.

Confinement may be a specific provocateur of self-injurious behavior for vulnerable persons.

Winchel & Stanley
(p. 313)

Feldman, M.D. (1988). The challenge of self-mutilation: A review. *Comprehensive Psychiatry, 29,* **252-269. (rank = 10)**
Outlines theoretical perspectives, clinical presentation in nonmentally ill, nonpsychotic patients. Briefly summarizes treatment studies, mostly anecdotal. 20+ studies.

Selected Positive Trial

van Moffaert, M. (1990). Management of self-mutilation: Confrontation and integration of psychotherapy and psychotropic drug treatment. *Psychotherapy and Psychosomatics, 51,* **180-186. (rank = 45)**

SEXUAL ABUSE (see also Child Abuse)

Major Research Reviews in Core Journals

Marshall, W.L., Jones, R., Ward, T., Johnston, P. et al (1991). Treatment outcome with sex offenders. *Clinical Psychology Review, 11,* 465-485. (rank = 3)
This paper reviews research on a variety of medical and psychological interventions, including psychosurgery, castration, pharmacotherapy, self-help programs, and behavioral treatment. Outpatient and institutional settings such as prisons and state hospitals are covered. The authors conclude that despite a general lack of rigor, this research yielded some encouraging findings, particularly with regard to cognitive-behavioral procedures for child abuse and exhibitionism.They note little success in the treatment of rape offenders. 20+ studies.

...behavior therapy procedures ...focus primarily on developing (or improving) adaptive sexual functioning and eliminating specific deviant behaviors, thoughts, and feelings.

Lanyon (p. 176)

Lanyon, R. (1986). Theory and treatment in child molestation. *Journal of Consulting and Clinical Psychology, 54,* 176-182. (rank = 1)
Lanyon presents a theoretical overview followed by a selective review of the treatment literature. The focus is on family systems and behavioral approaches to child molestation by males, excluding rape. The author concludes that at least one large-scale family systems program (N>4000 cases) proved highly effective for father-daughter incest and that behavior therapy, generally in-

volving covert desensitization, also produced promising results in more than a dozen controlled studies. A series of research-based treatment recommendations is included. 10+ studies.

Other Significant Reviews

MacMillan, H.L., MacMillan, J.H., Offord, D.R., Griffith, L. et al (1994). Primary prevention of child sexual abuse: A critical review. Part II. *Journal of Child Psychology and Psychiatry and Allied Disciplines 35*, 857-876. (rank = 8)
Reviews controlled studies of educational programs for children, parents, teachers. Most observed increase in knowledge, none examined effect on occurrence of abuse. Partially supported by grant from Canadian government. 19 studies.

There is widespread enthusiasm for the use of group therapy in the treatment of CSA victims.

Cahill et al (p. 6)

Cahill, C., Llewelyn, S.P., & Pearson, C. (1991). Treatment of sexual abuse that occurred in childhood: A review. *British Journal of Clinical Psychology, 30*, 1-12. (rank = 29)
Describes mostly case studies, brief group treatment for adult women. Cites one evaluation of long-term group. Sessions < 12 12+ studies.

Kolko, D.J. (1988). Educational programs to promote awareness and prevention of child sexual victimization: A review and methodological critique. *Clinical Psychology Review, 8*, 195-209. (rank = 3)
Highlights effectiveness data on programs for

teachers, parents, child care workers, direct classroom instruction. 10+ studies.

Miller-Perrin, C.L., & Wurtele, S.K. (1988). The child sexual abuse prevention movement: A critical analysis of primary and secondary approaches. *Clinical Psychology Review, 8,* 313-329. (rank = 3)
Detailed review of findings on primary prevention (implemented prior to abuse) and secondary prevention (implemented as early as possible after abuse). 10+ studies.

The prevalence of erectile difficulties increases to over 60% in men over 65...

Mohr & Beutler (p. 123)

Selected Positive Trial

Follette, V.M., Alexander, P.C., & Follette, W.C. (1991). Individual predictors of outcome in group treatment for incest survivors. *Journal of Consulting and Clinical Psychology, 59,* 150-155. (rank = 1)

SEXUAL DISORDERS

Major Research Reviews in Core Journals

Mohr, D.C., & Beutler, L.E. (1990). Erectile dysfunction: A review of diagnostic and treatment procedures. *Clinical Psychology Review, 10,* 123-150. (rank = 3)
Most of the reviewed investigations tested cognitive-behavioral, multimodal, or Masters and Johnson-type procedures. These included system-

atic desensitization, hypnotherapy, and communication and social skills training. Although several used large patient samples and follow-up periods to 8 years, few were well-controlled. Nonetheless, the authors consider results promising, with approximately two-thirds of patients expressing satisfaction with treatment across reports. Group techniques were found to be effective in several studies. 20+ studies.

Primary organismic dysfunction in women responds well to directed masturbation training programs.

LoPiccolo, J., & Stock, W.E. (1986). Treatment of sexual dysfunction. *Journal of Consulting and Clinical Psychology, 54,* 158-167. (rank = 1)

LoPiccolo & Stock (p. 158)

LoPiccolo and Stock provide a broad overview of treatment and research issues. Not intended as a comprehensive review, the paper nevertheless describes and briefly evaluates more than a dozen clinical reports, most case studies or uncontrolled designs. The authors conclude that success rates were highest for premature ejaculation. Like Cole (1985) below, they find much of the literature difficult to interpret due to methodological shortcomings. Self-help and group methods appeared to be effective with selected patients. 12+ studies.

Cole, M. (1985). Sex therapy: A critical appraisal. *British Journal of Psychiatry, 147,* 337-351. (rank = 6)

Cole reviews mostly behavioral outcome reports on erectile dysfunction, premature ejaculation, and vaginismus. Two psychodynamic investigations are also cited, one a large-scale study of some 100 patients. Despite success rates exceeding 50% in some studies, the author interprets results as "not very reassuring" due to flawed research methods as well as the complex social and biological etiology of these disorders. 12+ studies.

Few authors have faced the reality that all things are not possible; sex therapy has intrinsic limitations.

Cole
(p. 349)

Other Significant Reviews

McCabe, M.P., & Delaney, S.M. (1992). An evaluation of therapeutic programs for the treatment of secondary inorgasmia in women. *Archives of Sexual Behavior, 21,* 69-89. (rank = 26)
Overview of case reports on sexual problems related to medical, psychiatric disorders, poor communication skills, marital distress, sexual anxiety. 20+ studies.

Brown, G.R. (1990). A review of clinical approaches to gender dysphoria. *Journal of Clinical Psychiatry, 51,* 57-64. (rank = 5)
Surveys clinical studies of transsexualism, other forms of gender dysphoria. Includes discussion of psychotherapy, hormonal, surgical procedures. 30+ studies.

Selected Positive Trial

Hawton, K., Catalan, J., & Fagg, J. (1992). Sex therapy for erectile dysfunction: Characteristics of couples, treatment outcome, and prognostic factors.

Archives of Sexual Behavior, 21, 161-175.
(rank = 26)

SLEEP DISORDERS

Major Research Reviews in Core Journals

Morin, C.M., Culbert, J.P., & Schwartz, S.M. (1994). Nonpharmacological interventions for insomnia: A meta-analysis of treatment efficacy. *American Journal of Psychiatry, 151,* 1172-1180. **(rank = 2)**
Morin et al evaluate research on the behavioral treatment of insomnia. They conclude that behavioral methods produced reliable symptomatic improvement across studies, often with long-standing sleep complaints (mean duration = 11 years). Stimulus control and sleep restriction procedures proved most effective. Supported by a grant from the National Institute of Mental Health. [See Lacks & Morin (1992) and Turner (1986) below for narrative reviews of this literature.] Effect size = .9 60 studies.

France, K.G., & Hudson, S.M. (1993). Management of infant sleep disturbance: A review. *Clinical Psychology Review, 13,* 635-647. **(rank = 3)**
The major approach to infant sleep problems involves scheduled awakenings, stimulus control, and extinction, the most commonly used procedure. Case reports and uncontrolled single-

Infant sleep disturbance is a commonly reported problem, affecting 15-35% of infants...

France & Hudson (p. 635)

group studies make up the bulk of the research literature. The authors find results encouraging, particularly with regard to extinction-based procedures. A brief review of pharmacotherapy, highlighting evidence of limited shortterm effectiveness, is included. 24 studies.

The experimental analysis of the efficacy of behavioral self-control techniques for the treatment of insomnia is methodologically exemplary. Sound designs with control groups are the norm.

Turner (p. 27)

Lacks, P., & Morin, C.M. (1992). Recent advances in the assessment and treatment of insomnia. *Journal of Consulting and Clinical Psychology, 60,* 586-594. (rank = 1)
This state-of-the-art review considers outcome studies of behavioral, cognitive, and multi-component treatments for sleep-onset and maintenance complaints. Stimulus control procedures are seen as most effective, with approximately two-thirds of patients on average experiencing at least a 50% reduction in symptoms at follow-up periods of up to 1 year. Group administration in ten reports proved inferior to individual therapy. Sessions < 12 17 studies.

Turner, R.M. (1986). Behavioral self-control procedures for disorders of initiating and maintaining sleep (DIMS). *Clinical Psychology Review, 6,* 27-38. (rank = 3)
Turner reviews research on four procedures for insomnia and related sleep disorders. These are progressive and biofeedback-assisted relaxation; stimulus control methods designed to reassociate the bed as a cue to sleep; and paradoxical in-

tention, a cognitive technique for reducing the worry connected with loss of sleep. The author concludes that evidence was strongest for progressive relaxation, with well-designed studies demonstrating positive results on both self-report and physiological measures. Biofeedback and stimulus control procedures also scored successes in controlled investigations. Results with paradoxical methods were generally inconsistent across trials. Sessions < 12 25+ studies.

Selected Positive Trial

Morin, C.M., Stone, J., McDonald, K., & Jones, S. (1994). Psychological management of insomnia: A clinical replication series with 100 patients. *Behavior Therapy, 25,* **291-309. (rank = 7)**

...when nicotine gum is used as the main or sole treatment strategy, its initial effectiveness dissipates over time.

Cepeda-Benito
(p. 826)

SMOKING

Major Research Reviews in Core Journals

Cepeda-Benito, A., (1993). Meta-analytical review of the efficacy of nicotine chewing gum in smoking treatment programs. *Journal of Consulting and Clinical Psychology, 61,* **822-830. (rank = 1)**
This meta-analysis focuses on investigations of nicotine gum used alone and in combination with psychoeducational methods. Results of the analysis indicate that nicotine gum used alone pro-

duced better shortterm outcomes than placebo. This advantage was lost, however, by 8-12 month follow-up, when abstinence rates for both groups dropped to roughly 10%. In contrast nicotine gum combined with psychoeducational procedures proved superior to placebo both at the end of treatment and at longer term assessment. Supported by a grant from the American Cancer Society. Effect size = .2 33 studies.

Self-help interventions are also cost-effective... ranging from $22 to $144 per quitter.

Curry (p. 790)

Curry, S.J., (1993). Self-help interventions for smoking cessation. *Journal of Consulting and Clinical Psychology, 61,* 790-803. (rank = 1)

Curry reviews outcome studies that evaluated the effectiveness of written self-help manuals. She concludes that despite lower quit rates in comparison with more intensive programs, self-help manuals offer a cost-effective means of reaching a large population of smokers. Supported by grants from the National Institute of Drug Abuse and the National Heart, Lung and Blood Institute. 24 studies.

Lichtenstein, E., & Glasgow, R.E. (1992). Smoking cessation: What have we learned over the past decade? *Journal of Consulting and Clinical Psychology, 60,* 518-527. (rank = 1)

Lichtenstein and Glasgow survey reports on an array of interventions including intensive clinic-based treatment, worksite programs, self-help, relapse prevention, and community-based media and classroom initiatives. They interpret results as generally promising for clinic-based and nicotine replacement strategies, mediocre for relapse prevention, and mixed for the other approaches considered. Supported by grants from the National Cancer Institute. 30+ studies.

Other Significant Reviews

Hughes, J.R. (1993). Pharmacotherapy for smoking cessation: Unvalidated assumptions, anomalies, and suggestions for future research. *Journal of Consulting and Clinical Psychology, 61,* 751-760. **(rank = 1)**
Analysis of research indicates psychological methods increased effectiveness of nicotine gum, effect on transdermal patch treatment not documented. Clinical decision-making, cost issues discussed. Supported by grant from National Institute on Drug Abuse. 40+ studies.

Carey, M.P., Snel, D.L., Carey, K.B., & Richards, C.S. (1989). Self-initiated smoking cessation: A review of the empirical literature from stress and coping perspectives. *Cognitive Therapy and Research, 13,* 323-341. **(rank = 13)**
Summarizes success predictors from studies of people who quit without professional help. Partially supported by grants from National Institute of Health, American Cancer Society. 23 studies.

...successful quitters generally are able to enlist the support of others, which in turn eases the discomfort of quitting.

Carey et al (p. 338)

Glasgow, R.E., & Lichtenstein, E. (1987). Long-term effects of behavioral smoking cessation interventions. *Behavior Therapy, 18,* 297-324. (rank = 7)
Finds 1-year quit rates of 40% for strongest behavioral programs, greater than 25% at 2-6 year follow-up. Partially supported by unspecified federal grants. 30+ studies.

the relative effectiveness of group versus individual treatment is an important question for consideration...

Heimberg (p. 125)

Selected Positive Trial

Killen, J.D., Fortmann, S.P., Newman, B, & Varady, A. (1990). Evaluation of a treatment approach combining nicotine gum with self-guided behavioral treatments for smoking relapse prevention. *Journal of Consulting and Clinical Psychology, 58,* 85-92. (rank = 1)

SOCIAL PHOBIA (see also Anxiety Disorders)

Major Research Reviews in Core Journals

Heimberg, R.G. (1989). Cognitive and behavioral treatments for social phobia: A critical analysis. *Clinical Psychology Review, 9,* 107-128. (rank = 3)
Heimberg evaluates treatment research on a variety of social phobias including fear of speaking, fear of writing or eating in public, and various performance anxieties. Social skills training, exposure, relaxation, and cognitive restructuring

techniques were the primary modes of therapy investigated. Treatment was brief and often delivered in groups. The author interprets results as supporting these methods, albeit inconclusively, given the absence of adequate controls in most of the research discussed. Sessions < 12 12 studies.

Liebowitz, M.R., Gorman, J.M., Fyer, A.J., & Klein, D.F. (1985). Social phobia: Review of a neglected anxiety disorder. *Archives of General Psychiatry,* **42, 729-736. (rank = 1)**

This paper presents a detailed introduction to social phobias including epidemiology, assessment, differential diagnosis, the relation to panic disorder and other phobias, and treatment effectiveness research. Pharmacological and behavioral outcome studies are reviewed. The authors conclude that data from analogue and a very few controlled studies pointed to the moderate efficacy of beta-blockers, particularly with performance anxiety, and the possible benefit of monoamine oxidase inhibitors in selected cases. Behavioral procedures such as desensitization, social skills training, and cognitive restructuring yielded modest to substantial improvement rates. Partially supported by grants from the National Institute of Mental Health. 20+ studies.

The disorder is not uncommon and tends to be chronic and at times disabling. Alcoholism and depression are common associated syndromes.

Liebowitz et al (p. 735)

Other Significant Reviews

Donohue, B.C., van Hasselt, V.B., & Hersen, M. (1994). Behavioral assessment and treatment of social phobia. *Behavior Modification, 18,* 262-288. (rank = 28)

Reviews outcome studies of social skills training, relaxation procedures, exposure, cognitive therapy. Notes some positive findings, generally inconclusive results. 20+ studies.

Selected Positive Trial

Turner, S.M., Beidel, D.C., & Jacob R.G. (1994) Social phobia: A comparison of behavior therapy and atenolol. *Journal of Consulting and Clinical Psychology, 62,* 350-358. (rank = 1)

For most chronically mentally ill patients who remain at risk, particularly schizophrenic patients, when the intervention ends, so does the effect.

Hogarty (p. 368)

SOCIAL WORK

Major Research Reviews in Core Journals

Hogarty, G.E. (1989). Meta-analysis of the effects of practice with the chronically mentally ill: A critique and reappraisal of the literature. *Social Work, 34,* 363-373. (rank = 2)

Hogarty offers detailed criticism of Videka-Sherman (1988) below, particularly with respect to the benefits of time-limited versus long-term treatments. He also presents outcome data supporting the combination of psychosocial, pharmacologic, and community care in the treatment of schizophrenia. 5+ studies.

Videka-Sherman, L. (1988). Meta-analysis of research on social work practice in mental health. *Social Work, 33,* **325-338. (rank = 2)**
This is a two-part meta-analysis of social work outcome studies. In the first part, Videka-Sherman evaluates individual, group, and family methods for typical outpatient complaints in community agencies. The other analysis examines outcome data on community-based treatment for the chronic mentally ill. For the most part, these were full-day programs for people suffering from schizophrenia, depression, and personality disorders. The author observes a modest treatment effect in both parts of the meta-analysis. She also notes that shorter term interventions appeared to produce greater gains than long-term methods with both acute and chronic populations. Partially supported by a grant from the National Association of Social Workers. [For a critique of this review see Hogarty (1989) above.] Effect size for typical outpatient care = .5 Effect size for chronic care = .3 30 studies, part 1; 23 studies, part 2.

In another successful program, an interdisciplinary team (psychiatrist, social worker, and psychologist) developed a home-visit-based family therapy program for schizophrenic clients and their families.

Videka-Sherman (p. 335)

Other Significant Reviews

Sheldon, B. (1986). Social work effectiveness experiments: Review and implications. *British Journal of Social Work, 16,* **223-42. (rank = 9)**

Reviews major evaluations of delinquency prevention, family interventions for at-risk children,
social skills training for elderly. Notes positive
findings. 5 studies.

*...chronic cocaine
users regularly
report increasing
dysphoria,
anxiety, a sense of
loss of control
...and confusion.*

*Weddington
(p. 88)*

Selected Positive Trial

**Mancoske, R.J., Standifer, D., & Cauley, C. (1994).
The effectiveness of brief counseling services for
battered women. *Research on Social Work Practice 4,* 53-63. (rank = 8)**

SUBSTANCE ABUSE – Standard Therapies

Major Research Reviews in Core Journals

**Weddington, W. (1993). Cocaine: Diagnosis and
treatment. *Psychiatric Clinics of North America, 16,*
87-95. (rank = 30)**
Weddington provides an introduction to cocaine
abuse that emphasizes physiological aspects, psychiatric comorbidity, and treatment. He reviews
several outcome studies, including two large-
scale investigations of inpatient Alcoholics Anonymous-type programs. One-year abstinence rates
approaching 50-60% were obtained, with at-
tendance at posttreatment aftercare emerging as
a predictor of success. Two outpatient studies
also reported modest improvement, one involving
a cognitive-behavioral contracting procedure, the

other a comparison between self-management and interpersonal psychotherapy. The author also notes several pharmacotherapy studies in progress. 5+ studies.

Platt, J.J., Husband, S.D., & Taube, D. (1990-91). Major psychotherapeutic modalities for heroin addiction. *International Journal of the Addictions, 25,* 1453-1477. (rank = 8)

This paper includes a broad survey of treatment studies and a discussion of the theoretical rationale underlying various psychological approaches to heroin addiction. Supportive psychotherapy, family therapy, behavioral treatment, and therapeutic communities, the most heavily researched approach, are covered. Several of the investigations used experimental designs. According to the authors, social skills training for adolescents and supportive psychotherapy for patients with high levels of psychopathology appeared to offer some promise, especially when used in conjunction with methadone treatment. Therapeutic communities reported some long-term successes but particularly high attrition rates. 10+ studies.

...legal pressure generally is important in influencing retention in therapeutic community programs...

Platt et al (p. 1467)

Other Significant Reviews

Maddux, J.F., & Desmond, D.P. (1992). Methadone maintenance and recovery from opioid dependence. *American Journal of Drug and Alcohol Abuse, 18,* 63-74. (rank = 4)

Analysis of outcome data indicates 9-21% abstinence rates for methadone programs, 10-19% for drug-free approaches 5+ years following discharge. Concludes methadone use did not impede eventual recovery. Supported by grant from National Institute on Drug Abuse. 5 methadone studies; 6 drug-free studies.

...therapeutic communities retrained their clients in fundamental living skills, including managing a bank account...

Peele (p.1412)

Peele, S. (1990-91). What works in addiction treatment and what doesn't: Is the best therapy no therapy? *International Journal of the Addictions, 25,* 1409-1419. (rank = 8)
Cites data challenging effectiveness of 12-step programs, disease model. Favors coping skills, cost-control approaches. 5 studies.

Gawin, F.H., & Ellinwood, E.H. (1988). Cocaine and other stimulants: Actions, abuse, and treatment. *New England Journal of Medicine, 318,* 1173-1182. (rank = 1)
Overview of epidemiology, psychiatric comorbidity, biological factors. Includes brief summary of drug, nondrug treatments. 10+ studies.

Allison, M., & Hubbard, R.L. (1985). Drug abuse treatment process: A review of the literature. *International Journal of the Addictions, 20,* 1321-1345. (rank = 8)
Briefly highlights studies on therapeutic communities, methadone programs, family, behavioral methods. Supported by grant from National Institute on Drug Abuse. 30+ studies.

Selected Positive Trial

Azrin, N.H., McMahon, P.T., Donohue, B., Besales, V.A. et al (1994). Behavior therapy for drug abuse: A controlled treatment outcome study. *Behaviour Research and Therapy, 32,* **857-866. (rank = 9)**

SUBSTANCE ABUSE – Dual Diagnosis

Major Research Reviews in Core Journals

Bickel, W.K., Marion, I., & Lowinson, J.H. (1987). The treatment of alcoholic methadone patients: A review. *Journal of Substance Abuse Treatment, 4,* **15-19. (rank = 6)**
Alcoholism is a significant problem for many narcotics addicts undergoing methadone treatment. This paper focuses on a handful of studies that attempted to reduce drinking in methadone patients. The authors observe that poor results were obtained in several investigations of disulfiram treatment, and in one study of insight-oriented and controlled drinking approaches, due to low patient motivation. Positive results are noted in two behavioral studies in which access to methadone was made contingent upon adherence to a disulfiram program. Supported by a grant from the National Institute on Alcohol Abuse and Alcoholism. 5+ studies.

Twenty-five percent of all discharges from methadone treatment are due to alcoholism or the disruptive behavior of patients under the influence.

Bickel et al (p. 15)

Other Significant Reviews

Salloum, I.M., Moss, H.B., & Daley, D.C. (1991). Substance abuse and schizophrenia: Impediments to optimal care. *American Journal of Drug and Alcohol Abuse, 17,* 321-336. (rank = 4)

Discusses prevalence, diagnosis, etiology, treatment. Finds few studies of psychotherapy, drug treatment, generally poor results. Disulfiram probably contraindicated due to exacerbation of psychotic symptoms. Partially supported by grants from National Institute on Alcohol Abuse and Alcoholism and National Institute on Drug Abuse. 5+ studies.

...relapse rates posttreatment are high, ranging from 35% to 85%.

Catalano et al (p. 1086)

Selected Positive Trial

Hoffman, G.W., DiRito, D.C., & McGill, E.C. (1993). Three-month follow-up of 28 dual diagnosis inpatients. *American Journal of Drug and Alcohol Abuse 19,* 79-88. (rank = 4)

SUBSTANCE ABUSE – Youth

Major Research Reviews in Core Journals

Catalano, R.F., Hawkins, J.D., Wells, E.A., Miller, J.L. et al (1990-91). Evaluation of the effectiveness of adolescent drug abuse treatment, assessment of risks for relapse, and promising approaches for re-

lapse prevention. *International Journal of the Addictions, 25,* 1085-1140. (rank = 8)
Catalano et al review findings on a variety of treatment programs. Reviewed studies covered inpatient psychodynamic therapy, cognitive-behavioral procedures, Alcoholics Anonymous-type programs, and school- and community-based strategies. Few investigations were well-controlled, although several did compare alternative treatments to waiting-list or other control conditions. Follow-up assessments ranging up to 4-6 years were reported. In light of the modestly superior outcomes obtained with therapy versus control procedures in some studies, Catalano et al conclude that "some treatment is better than no treatment." No clear differences in results were found among the various therapies. Partially supported by grants from the National Institute on Drug Abuse and the Office of Juvenile Justice and Delinquency Prevention. 16 studies.

As it stands, the public record shows that substance abuse education has, for the most part, failed to achieve its primary goal, the prevention of drug and alcohol abuse.

Bangert-Drowns (p. 260)

Bangert-Drowns, R.L. (1988). The effects of school-based substance abuse education: A meta-analysis. *Journal of Drug Education, 18,* 243-264. (rank = 10)
This meta-analysis evaluates results of drug and alcohol prevention programs carried out across a spectrum of educational settings from elementary school to college. All studies tested a prevention program against a no-treatment condition. Most were short, the majority less than 6

weeks in duration. Findings indicate these programs may have had modest success in enhancing knowledge but probably had little effect on attitudes and behavior related to drug and alcohol use. Effect size for knowledge = .8   Effect size for attitudes = .3 Effect size for behavior = .1   33 studies.

Preventive interventions in schools, homes, and communities are designed to modify everyday influences on children's and adolescents' substance use.

Schinke & Gilchrist (p. 597)

Tobler, N.S. (1986). Meta-analysis of 143 adolescent drug prevention programs: Quantitative outcome results of program participants compared to a control or comparison group. *Journal of Drug Issues, 16,* 537-567. (rank = 5)

Tobler assesses findings of adolescent prevention programs related to the use of drugs, alcohol, and tobacco. Most aimed at increasing knowledge, changing attitudes, or directly altering behavior. Overall, analysis of outcome data indicates a modest effect for peer-led interventions such as assertiveness or "refusal" training. The author concludes that programs devoted exclusively to increasing knowledge about substance abuse, rather than specific social skills, had only a minimal impact. A list of references to the studies covered by this meta-analysis is not included. Effect size = .3   100+ studies.

Schinke, S.P., & Gilchrist, L.B. (1985). Preventing substance abuse with children and adolescents. *Journal of Consulting and Clinical Psychology, 53,* 596-602. (rank = 1)

Schinke and Gilchrist describe preliminary efforts to map a research strategy for tobacco, alcohol, and drug abuse prevention. They highlight a handful of studies, mostly school-based, that focused on assertiveness, social skills, and problem-solving to enhance the student's ability to resist peer pressure. Although highly tentative, results of these early reports are seen as "hopeful, incremental beginnings." Supported by grants from the National Cancer Institute, the National Institute on Drug Abuse, and the W.T. Grant Foundation. 10+ studies.

...adolescent substance abuse is probably the most commonly missed pediatric diagnosis.

Bailey
(p. 155)

Other Significant Reviews

Farrell, M., & Strang, J. (1991). Substance use and misuse in childhood and adolescence. *Journal of Child Psychology and Psychiatry and Allied Disciplines, 32,* **109-128. (rank = 8)**
Overview of epidemiology, assessment, diagnostic issues. Describes longitudinal reports on natural history. No controlled outcome studies. 5+ studies.

Bailey, G.W. (1989). Current perspectives on substance abuse in youth. *Journal of the American Academy of Child and Adolescent Psychiatry, 28,* **151-162. (rank = 7)**
Considers outcome research on outpatient, inpatient, residential aftercare programs. Few controlled studies. Cites evaluation of "Just Say No" approach, minimally effective. 20+ studies.

Selected Positive Trial

Blood, L., & Cornwall, A., (1994). Pretreatment variables that predict completion of an adolescent substance abuse treatment program. *Journal of Nervous and Mental Disease, 182,* 14-19. (rank = 11)

The relatively sparse scientific research literature may also be entangled with elaborate claims of developers of CES devices.

Alling et al (p. 173)

SUBSTANCE ABUSE – Special Topics

Major Research Reviews in Core Journals

Brewington, V., Smith, M., & Lipton, D. (1994). Acupuncture as a detoxification treatment: An analysis of controlled research. *Journal of Substance Abuse Treatment, 11,* 289-307. (rank = 6)
This paper reviews outcome data, anecdotal reports, laboratory studies, and animal research bearing on the usefulness of acupuncture in the treatment of substance abuse. Although the bulk of outcome studies did not include placebo controls, the authors conclude that overall findings supported a limited role for acupuncture in alcohol, opiate, and tobacco withdrawal.
20+ studies.

Alling, F.A., Johnson, E.D., & Elmoghazy, E. (1990). Cranial electrostimulation (CES) use in the detoxification of opiate-dependent patients. *Journal of Substance Abuse Treatment, 7,* 173-180. (rank = 6)

In cranial electrostimulation a mild or non-detectable electrical current is applied across the skin surface of the head. The procedure is used to reduce subjective discomfort and other withdrawal symptoms during opiate detoxification. Alling et al examine controlled studies as well as proposed mechanisms of action. Based on the positive findings of several double-blind and placebo-controlled reports, the authors conclude CES may be a "promising line of inquiry." 5+ studies.

These studies also concluded that there is substantial evidence that... inpatient treatment is not superior to outpatient care, and that inpatient treatment is far more expensive.

Allen & Phillips (p. 753)

Other Significant Reviews

Allen, M.G., & Phillips, K.L. (1993). Utilization review of treatment for chemical dependence. *Hospital and Community Psychiatry, 44,* 752-756. **(rank = 19)**
Short summary of treatment research that favored outpatient over inpatient care except when danger to self or others, coexisting physical or psychiatric disorder, nonresponse to adequate outpatient trial. Provides detailed guidelines, case examples for utilization review. 5+ studies.

Stark, M.J. (1992). Dropping out of substance abuse treatment: A clinically oriented review. *Clinical Psychology Review, 12,* 93-116. **(rank = 3)**
Concludes outcomes significantly worse for early dropouts, attrition rates lower with smaller treatment groups, higher staff ratios. 30+ studies.

Selected Positive Trial

Carlson, H.B., Dilts, S.L., & Radcliff, S. (1994). Physicians with substance abuse problems and their recovery environment: A survey. ***Journal of Substance Abuse Treatment, 11,* 113-119.** **(rank = 6)**

It is probably a mistake to dismiss hotlines as well-intentioned but ineffective.

Shaffer et al (p. 683)

SUICIDE

Major Research Reviews in Core Journals

Shaffer, D., Garland, A., Gould, M., Fisher, P. et al (1988). Preventing teenage suicide: A critical review. ***Journal of the American Academy of Child and Adolescent Psychiatry, 27,* 675-687.** **(rank = 7)**
This paper provides a detailed review of research on a variety of suicide-related programs. These include school-based prevention, hotline and crisis services, postemergency room counseling, and survivor groups. Studies of programs for teenagers, college students, and adults are considered. Most were poorly controlled. The authors note a dearth of documented successes in general but conclude that efforts aimed at high risk groups showed some promise. Partially supported by grants from the Centers for Disease Control and the National Institute of Mental Health. 10+ studies.

Selected Positive Trial

Linehan, M.M., Heard, H.L., & Armstrong, H.E. (1993). Naturalistic follow-up of a behavioral treatment for chronically parasuicidal borderline patients. *Archives of General Psychiatry, 50*, 971-974. (rank = 1)

TYPE A BEHAVIOR PATTERN (see also Heart Disease, Hypertension)

Major Research Reviews in Core Journals

Thoresen, C.E., & Powell, L.H. (1992). Type A behavior pattern: New perspectives on theory, assessment and intervention. *Journal of Consulting and Clinical Psychology, 60*, 595-604. (rank = 1)
As part of a general overview of theory and research, Thoresen and Powell summarize previous reviews and selectively critique some of the recent treatment literature. They conclude that efforts to modify Type A behavior generally yielded improvements in psychosocial and/or cardiovascular functioning. Several reports, including at least one large-scale well-controlled trial, documented positive effects on physiological and disease measures such as coronary mortality. 5+ studies.

The encouraging results of controlled interventions contrast sharply with the often inconsistent results of correlational designs.

Thoresen & Powell
(p. 601)

Haaga, D.A. (1987). Treatment of the Type A behavior pattern. *Clinical Psychology Review, 7,* 557-574. (rank = 3)

Haaga presents a comprehensive review of outcome research on behavioral techniques used to alter Type A behavior. Postmyocardial infarction patients and healthy but coronary-prone volunteers were the target populations in most studies. Interventions were generally brief, typically less than 10 sessions. Results supported the superiority of multifaceted behavioral treatments to control procedures such as relaxation training and aerobics in reducing cardiac recurrence rates in heart patients. It was not clear that treatment had a significant impact on the development or course of heart disease in coronary-prone volunteers. 20+ studies.

Type A people show greater sympathetic nervous system activity than do Type B...

Haaga (p. 557)

Nunes, E.V., Frank, K.A., & Kornfeld, D.S. (1987). Psychologic treatment for the Type A behavior pattern and for coronary heart disease: A meta-analysis of the literature. *Psychosomatic Medicine, 48,* 159-173. (rank = 4)

This paper primarily evaluates the impact of behavioral and psychoeducational procedures on middle-aged postinfarction patients. Most procedures were administered in groups, with an average duration of 8-21 hours. The most intensive (and arguably most successful) trial, however, involved more than 100 treatment hours. Nunes et al conclude that across trials these procedures produced moderate shortterm reductions in Type A behavior. The effect on heart disease was less clearcut, although two trials did document a roughly 50% decline in coronary events at 3-year follow-up. Effect size = .6 10 studies.

Selected Positive Trial

Roskies, E., Seraganian, P., Oseasohn, R., Hanley, J.A. et al (1986). The Montreal Type A intervention project: Major findings. *Health Psychology, 5,* 45-69. (rank = 8)

These data also suggest that the impact of treatment on CHD is less evident at 1 year and more evident at 3 years.

Nunes et al (p. 169)

SUMMARY TABLES

1 Treatments Receiving Strong Support in Meta-Analyses

2 Treatments Receiving Marginal Support in Meta-Analyses

3 Treatments Receiving Marginal Support in Non-Meta-Analytic Reviews

4 Comparative Effectiveness of Drug and Nondrug Procedures

5 Comparative Effectiveness of Group and Individual Procedures

6 Treatments with an Average Duration under 12 Sessions

7 Treatments Showing a Weak Correlation between Duration and Outcome

8 Treatments for which Research-Based Guidelines are Provided in Reviews

9 Meta-Analyses

table 1   145

TABLE 1

Treatments Receiving Strong Support in Meta-Analyses[1]

Cognitive and/or
behavior therapy

bulimia	Hartmann et al	47
conduct disorder	Durlak	27
depression	Dobson	32
impulsivity	Baer & Nietzel	14
insomnia	Morin et al	119
obsessive-compulsive disorder	Christensen et al	81
panic disorder	Clum et al	89
	Cox et al	91

Drug therapy

obsessive-compulsive disorder	Christensen et al	81
panic disorder	Clum et al	89
	Cox et al	91

Electroconvulsive therapy	Parker et al	41

General psychotherapy

bulimia	Laessle et al	40
geriatric depression	Scogin & McElreath	49

Psychodynamic therapy (brief, manual-based)	Crits-Christoph	102
Rational emotive therapy	Engels et al	104
Relaxation training	Carlson & Hoyle	106

[1] Strong support is defined as yielding an effect size greater than .7, following guidelines suggested by researchers on meta-analysis [e.g. Wolf, F.M. (1986). *Meta-analysis: Quantitative methods for research synthesis*. Beverly Hills: Sage].

TABLE 2

Treatments Receiving Marginal Support
in Meta-Analyses[1]

Alcoholism counseling	*Agosti*[2]	3
Nicotine gum	*Cepeda-Benito*	121
Parent effectiveness training	*Cedar & Levant*	95
Psychodynamic therapy (brief)	*Svartberg & Stiles*[2]	103
Social work interventions *chronic mental illness*	*Videka-Sherman*	127
Substance abuse prevention	*Bangert-Drowns* *Tobler*	133 134

[1]Marginal support is defined as yielding an effect size less than .4, following guidelines suggested by researchers on meta-analysis [e.g. Wolf, F.M. (1986). *Meta-analysis: Quantitative methods for research synthesis.* Beverly Hills: Sage].

[2]Indicates use of an alternative method to calculate effect size.

table 3   147

TABLE 3

Treatments Receiving Marginal Support in
Non-Meta-Analytic Reviews

Alcoholism counseling	*Nathan & Skinstad*	*5*
Alcoholism prevention	*Meyer & Kranzler*	*4*
Aversion therapy		
alcohol abuse	*Elkins*	*6*
self-injury	*Blair*	*112*
Benzodiazepine therapy		
panic disorder	*Michelson & Marchione*	*90*
	Mattick et al	*92*
Biofeedback		
chemotherapy	*Carey & Burish*	*18*
hypertension	*Jacob et al*	*62*
	Johnston	*60*
Case management		
geriatric disorders	*McCallion et al*	*69*
Child therapy		
divorce	*Grych & Fincham*	*44*
Child therapy	*Shirk & Russell*	*25*
(nonbehavioral)	*Barrnett et al*	*22*
Cognitive-behavioral therapy		
preadolescent disorders	*Durlak et al*	*27*
Cognitive rehabilitation		
head injury	*Benedict*	*56*
Cognitive training		
attention-deficit hyperactivity	*Abikoff*	*13*

(continued)

Drug therapy
personality disorders	*Stone*	*96*
schizophrenia	*McGlashan*	*110*

General psychotherapy
personality disorders	*Stone*	*96*
schizophrenia	*McGlashan*	*110*

Group therapy
personality disorders	*Higgitt & Fonagy*	*97*

Hormonal therapy
premenstrual syndrome	*Robinson & Garfinkel*	*101*
	Blumenthal & Nadelson	*101*

Psychodynamic therapy
schizophrenia	*Mueser & Berenbaum*	*108*

Sex therapy	*Cole*	*117*

Sexual orientation counseling	*Haldeman*	*61*

Social skills training
conduct disorder	*Webster-Stratton*	*28*

Substance abuse counseling	*Allen & Phillips*	*137*
	Salloum et al	*132*
	Peele	*130*
	Bickel et al	*131*

Suicide counseling	*Shaffer et al*	*138*

Type A behavior modification	*Haaga*	*140*

Weight-loss programs	*Garner & Wooley*	*77*
	Smith & Fremou	*79*

table 4   149

TABLE 4

Comparative Effectiveness of Drug
and Nondrug Procedures

Attention-deficit hyperactivity	*Dulcan*	*13*
	Gadow	*15*
Depression	*Conte et al*	*34*
	Hollon et al	*30, 31*
	Howland	*41*
	Robins & Hayes	*30*
	Conte & Karasu	*41*
	Robinson et al	*31*
	Dobson	*32*
	Meterissian & Bradwejn	*34*
	Wulsin	*38*
Eating disorders	*Abbott & Mitchell*	*47*
	Wilson & Fairburn	*45*
	Walsh & Devlin	*47*
	Laessle et al	*49*
Enuresis	*Houts et al*	*52*
Headache	*Holroyd & Penzien*	*58*
Obsessive-compulsive disorder	*Jenike & Rauch*	*82*
	van Blakom et al	*80*
	Abel	*82*
	Zetin & Kramer	*83*
	Christensen et al	*81*
Panic disorder	*Cox et al*	*91*
	Michelson & Marchione	*90*
	Mattick et al	*92*
	Clum	*92*
	Clum et al	*89*
	Marks & O'Sullivan	*91*
	Lydiard & Ballenger	*93*
Posttraumatic stress	*Solomon et al*	*98*
Self-injury	*Blair*	*112*

TABLE 5

Comparative Effectiveness of Group
and Individual Procedures

Alcoholism counseling	*Jarvis*	5
Child therapy	*Weisz et al*	23
	Casey & Berman	24

Cognitive and/or
behavior therapy

depression	*Scogin & McElreath*	40
	Robinson et al	31
	Nietzel et al	33
eating disorders	*Hartmann et al*	47
	Mitchell	48
	Cox & Merkel	48
irritable bowel syndrome	*Blanchard et al*	55
memory disorders	*Godfrey & Knight*	75
panic disorder	*Michelson & Marchione*	90
personality disorders	*Higgitt & Fonagy*	97
sexual disorders	*Mohr & Beutler*	116
	LoPicolo & Stock	117
sleep disorders	*Lacks & Morin*	120
social phobia	*Heimberg*	124

General psychotherapy

depression	*Robinson et al*	31
personality disorders	*Higgitt & Fonagy*	97

Group therapy

depression	*Wulsin et al*	38
posttraumatic stress	*Allen & Bloom*	99

Relaxation training	*Carlson & Hoyle*	106

table 6   151

TABLE 6

Treatments with an Average Duration
under 12 Sessions

Child therapy

divorce	Grych & Fincham	44
high risk neonates	McGuire & Earls	25
varied disorders	Casey & Berman	24

Cognitive and/or
behavior therapy

anxiety	Berman & Miller	9
arthritis	Young	11
attention-deficit hyperactivity	Abikoff	13
	Baer & Nietzel	14
cancer	Andersen	17
	Carey & Burish	18
	Telch & Telch	18
conduct disorder	Dumas	27
	Durlak	27
depression	Scogin & McElreath	40
	Robinson et al	31
	Dobson	32
	Conte & Plutchik	34
headache	Blanchard	55
	Holroyd & Penzien	58
irritable bowel syndrome	Blanchard et al	57
nightmares	Halliday	77
obsessive-compulsive disorder	Christensen et al	81
panic disorder	Marks & O'Sullivan	91
schizophrenia	Benton & Schroeder	107
sleep disorders	Lacks & Morin	120
	Turner	120
social phobia	Heimberg	124
Type A behavior	Haaga	140

(continued)

Electroconvulsive therapy	*Mukherjee & Sackheim*	*49*
Exercise therapy		
depression	*Simons & Epstein*	*37*
Group therapy		
cancer support	*Andersen*	*17*
	Telch & Telch	*18*
sexual abuse	*Cahill & Llewellyn*	*115*
Type A behavior	*Haaga*	*140*
Rational emotive therapy	*Lyons & Woods*	*105*
Relaxation training	*Carlson & Hoyle*	*106*

table 7   153

TABLE 7

Treatments Showing a Weak Correlation between
Duration and Outcome

Cognitive and/or
behavior therapy
    depression

depression	*Robinson et al*	*31*
	Dobson	*32*
eating disorders	*Cox et al*	*48*
	Nietzel & Russell	*33*

Social work interventions
    acute/chronic mental illness   *Videka-Sherman*   *127*

TABLE 8

Treatments for which Research-Based
Guidelines are Provided in Reviews

Biofeedback
 attention-deficit hyperactivity *Lubar*   14

Cognitive and/or
behavior therapy
 depression/panic   *Yager*   46
 eating disorders   *Laberge et al* 41
 obsessive-compulsive disorder *Jenike & Rauch* 82
          Jenike   83
 sexual abuse   *Lanyon*   114
 smoking   *Hughes*   123

Drug therapy
 adolescent anxiety   *Biederman* 10
 depression   *Paykel*   35
 eating disorders   *Yager*   46
 obsessive-compulsive disorder *Zetin & Kramer* 83
 schizophrenia   *McClellan & Werry* 110

Electroconvulsive therapy   *Monroe*   50
          Paykel   35

General psychotherapy
 depression   *Weissman & Markowitz* 36
 eating disorders   *Paykel*   35
          Yager   46

Interpersonal psychotherapy *Markowitz* 39

Substance abuse counseling   *Allen & Phillips* 137

table 9   155

TABLE 9

Meta-Analyses

Child therapy   *Weisz et al*   *23*
                                       Casey & Berman   *24*

Cognitive and/or
behavior therapy
  anxiety   *Chambless & Gillis*   *8*
  conduct disorder   *Durlak et al*   *27*
  depression   *Scogin & McElreath*   *40*
                                       Robinson et al   *31*
                                       Dobson   *32*
  eating disorders   *Hartmann et al*   *47*
                                       Laessle et al   *49*
  geriatric disorders   *Okun et al*   *63*
  impulsivity   *Baer & Nietzel*   *14*
  insomnia   *Morin et al*   *119*
  obsessive-compulsive disorder *van Blakom et al*   *80*
                                       Christensen et al   *81*
  pain   *Flor et al*   *86*
                                       Malone & Strube   *87*
  panic disorder   *Clum et al*   *89*
                                       Cox et al   *91*
  schizophrenia   *Benton & Schroeder*   *107*

Electroconvulsive therapy   *Parker et al*   *41*

Marital and family therapy   *Shadish et al*   *70*
                                       Hahlweig & Markman   *70*
                                       Hazelrigg et al   *71*
                                       Giblin et al   *73*

Meditation   *Eppley & Abrams*   *106*

(continued)

APPENDICES

1   Seminal Reviews of Psychotherapy Effectiveness

2   Selected Papers on Cost-Effectiveness

3   Selected Papers on Treatment Duration and Outcome

APPENDIX 1

Seminal Reviews of Psychotherapy Effectiveness

Eysenck, H.J. (1952). The effects of psychotherapy: An evaluation. *Journal of Consulting Psychology, 16,* 319-324. (rank=1) Eysenck examined the results of 19 studies published between 1927 and 1945 in this landmark paper. More than 7,000 inpatients and outpatients were involved, the majority suffering from neurotic disorders. These studies were, for the most part, uncontrolled and nonrigorous by current standards. Eysenck's analysis of results yielded his well-known "two-thirds" dictum, that "...roughly two-thirds of a group of neurotic patients will recover or improve to a marked extent within about two years of the onset of their illness, whether they are treated by means of psychotherapy or not" (p.322). This finding was hotly debated by Eysenck and others for at least the next two decades (see below).

Luborsky, L. (1954). A note on Eysenck's article, "The effects of psychotherapy: An evaluation." *British Journal of Psychology, 45,* 129-131. (rank=12)

Eysenck, H.J. (1954). A reply to Luborsky's note. *British Journal of Psychology, 45,* 132-133. (rank=12)

Strupp, H.H. (1964). The outcome problem in psychotherapy: A rejoinder. *Psychotherapy, 1,* 101. (rank=31)

Bergin, A.E., & Strupp, H.H. (1969). The last word (?) on psychotherapy research: A reply. *International Journal of Psychiatry, 7,* 160-168. (rank=23)

Luborsky, L., Singer, B., and Luborsky, L. (1975). Comparative studies of psychotherapies: Is it true that "everyone has won and all must have prizes"? *Archives of General Psychiatry, 32,* 995-1008. (rank=1)

(continued)

After Eysenck (1952) this was probably the second most influential review of psychotherapy effectiveness. Luborsky et al systematically evaluated findings of more than 50 controlled trials of drug treatment and psychotherapy, taking into account such variables as therapist experience, placebo credibility, treatment adequacy, and the possible effects of researcher allegiance on outcome. Results of this detailed analysis indicated that all forms of psychotherapy benefited significantly more patients than no treatment or minimal contact, that drug therapy produced greater gains than psychotherapy in a number of studies, and that combined treatment (drug plus psychotherapy) generally outperformed individual procedures. Luborsky et al's best known finding, however, was summarized in their "dodo bird" conclusion. Borrowing from the character in Alice in Wonderland who declared each of the entrants in a crazy quilt foot race the winner, the authors suggested that since all the traditional psychotherapies had proven effective, all should receive a prize.

Smith, M.L., & Glass, G.V. (1977). Meta-analysis of psychotherapy outcome studies. *American Psychologist, 32,* 752-760. **(rank=4)**
This was the last of the seminal reviews of psychotherapy and the first major application of the technique of meta-analysis in mental health. In this brief paper Smith and Glass integrated the findings of an immense research literature including nearly 400 controlled studies. Their conclusions echoed Luborsky et al's (1975) finding of equal effectiveness for the various therapies and, deriving an overall effect size of .68, explicitly challenged the negative assessment of Eysenck (1952).

APPENDIX 2

Selected Papers on Cost-Effectiveness

Sturm, R., & Wells, K.B. (1995). How can care for depression become more cost-effective? *JAMA: Journal of the American Medical Association, 273,* 51-58. (rank=4))
Analyzes simulation, empirical data for patients in HMO, multispecialty, small group, solo practices in three urban areas. Favors quality of care improvements rather than changes in specialty mix to increase cost-effectiveness.

Yates, B.T., Yokley, J.M., & Thomas, J.V. (1994). Cost-benefit analysis of six alternative payment incentives for child therapists. *Journal of Consulting and Clinical Psychology, 62,* 627-635. (rank=1)
Five-year study of monetary incentives to increase direct clinical service, reduce paperwork, other nonclinical tasks, county mental health agency. Results support cost-effectiveness of four incentive plans.

Grizenko, N., & Papineau, D. (1992). A comparison of the cost-effectiveness of day-treatment and residential treatment for children with severe behaviour problems. *Canadian Journal of Psychiatry, 37,* 393-400. (rank=28)
Retrospective comparison of residential versus day-treatment for 6-12 year olds, with oppositional, attention-deficit, adjustment, conduct disorders. Finds shorter stays, lower costs with day-treatment. Similar degree of improvement, reintegration into school, family for both groups. Supported by grant from Canadian government.

(continued)

Holder, H., Longabaugh, R., & Miller, W.R. (1991). The cost-effectiveness of treatment for alcoholism: A first approximation. *Journal of Studies on Alcohol, 52,* 517-540. (rank=2)
Evaluates outcome, cost data from numerous clinical trials, varied treatment settings, interventions. Finds support for social skills, self-control training, other inexpensive procedures. Negative relationship between cost and effectiveness. Partially supported by grant from National Institute on Alcohol Abuse and Alcoholism.

Coursey, R.D., Ward-Alexander, L., & Katz, B. (1990). Cost-effectiveness of providing insurance benefits for posthospital psychiatric halfway house stays. *American Psychologist, 45,* 1118-1126. (rank=4)
Controlled trial of insurance coverage for halfway house care following hospital discharge. Schizophrenia, depression, personality disorder most common diagnosis. Finds significant decrease in rate, length of rehospitalization, 50% reduction in hospital costs. Supported by grant from Blue Cross and Blue Shield.

APPENDIX 3

Selected Papers on Treatment Duration and Outcome

Condelli, W.S., & Hubbard, R.L. (1994). Relationship between time spent in treatment and client outcomes from therapeutic communities. *Journal of Substance Abuse Treatment, 11,* 25-33. (rank=6)
Analyzes outcomes for nearly 2,000 drug users in 10 private therapeutic communities, average stay 6.5 months. Reports approximately 40% pre-post reduction in number using opiods, arrested during follow-up year. Positive relationship between length of stay and outcome.

Herron, W.G., Eisenstadt, E.N., Javier, R.A., Primavera, L.H. et al (1994). Session effects, comparability, and managed care in the psychotherapies. *Psychotherapy, 31,* 279-285. (rank=31)
Reviews dose-effect research, studies of shortterm versus long-term therapy. Concludes 25-30 sessions optimum before initial progress review.

Steenbarger, B.N. (1994). Duration and outcome in psychotherapy: An integrative review. *Professional Psychology: Research and Practice, 25,* 111-119. (rank=27)
Summarizes results of reviews, individual trials. Finds relationship between outcome and duration only for certain patient subgroups.

Appleby, L., Desai, P.N., Luchins, D.J., Gibbons, R.D. et al (1993). Length of stay and recidivism in schizophrenia: A study of public psychiatric hospital patients. *American Journal of Psychiatry, 150,* 72-76. (rank=2)
Evaluates rehospitalization data for 1500 patients at 10 state hospitals. Notes 37% recidivism rate within 6 months for

(continued)

brief-stay patients (hospitalized less than 15 days) versus 29% for patients treated more than 30 days. Concludes brief stay generally appropriate except for small group requiring alternative care.

Barkham, M., Moorey, J., & Davis, G. (1992). Cognitive-behavioural therapy in two-plus-one sessions: A pilot field trial. *Behavioural Psychotherapy, 20,* 147-154. (rank=41)
Reports on controlled trial of three-session cognitive procedure. Two highly focused weekly sessions followed by final session 3 months later. Data indicate modest improvement with mild-moderate depression, patient acceptance of brief approach.

Flint, A.J. (1992). The optimum duration of antidepressant treatment in the elderly. *International Journal of Geriatric Psychiatry, 7,* 617-619. (rank=22)
Reviews findings on posttreatment course of depression in people over 60. Cites high recurrence risk for 2 years following treatment. Argues for continued antidepressant therapy beyond usual 6-month postremission period.

Howard, K.I., Kopta, S.M., Krause, M.S., & Orlinsky, D.E. (1986). The dose-effect relationship in psychotherapy. *American Psychologist, 41,* 159-164. (rank=4)
Meta-analytic evaluation of outcome, length-of-treatment data from 15 outpatient studies. Concludes 50% of patients measurably improved by 8 sessions, 75% by 26 sessions. See Phillips (1988) below for commentary on study limitations, implications.

Phillips, E.L. (1988). Length of psychotherapy and outcome: Observations stimulated by Howard, Kopta, Krause, and Orlinsky. *American Psychologist, 43,* 669-670. (rank=4)

AUTHOR INDEX

Windholz, M.J., 16
Wing, R., 62, 78, 80
Winston, A., 98
Wolf, D.A., 21
Wolfe, D., 19, 20
Woods, P.J., 105
Wooley, S.C., 77
Wulsin, L., 38
Wurtele, S.K., 116

Y

Yager, J., 46
Yoshikawa, H., 67
Young, A.S., 109
Young, L.D., 11

Z

Zetin, M., 83
Zimet, S.G., 66
Zoettl, C., 49

TREATMENT INDEX

DISORDER INDEX

POPULATION INDEX